Gr€€n from Green II
(Businesses & Utilities)

Profiting From The Energy Transition

Jim Houlihan

Green from Green II © Copyright 2024 by Jim Houlihan

ISBN 9798333909657

ISBN TBA (eBook)

All rights reserved

The content contained within this book may not be reproduced, duplicated or transmitted without direct written permission from the author or the publisher.

Under no circumstances will any blame or legal responsibility be held against the publisher, or author, for any damages, reparation, or monetary loss due to the information contained within this book, either directly or indirectly.

Legal Notice

This book is copyright protected. It is only for personal use. You cannot amend, distribute, sell, use, quote or paraphrase any part, or the content within this book, without the consent of the author or publisher.

Disclaimer Notice

Please note the information contained within this document is for educational and entertainment purposes only. All efforts have been executed to present accurate, up-to-date, reliable, and complete information. No warranties of any kind are declared or implied. Readers acknowledge that the author is not engaged in rendering legal, financial, medical or professional advice. The content within this book has been derived from various sources. Please consult a licensed professional before attempting any techniques outlined in this book.

By reading this document, the reader agrees that under no circumstances is the author responsible for any direct or indirect losses incurred because of the use of the information contained within this document, including, but not limited to, errors, omissions, or inaccuracies.

Book design by Jim Houlihan

Published by Jim Houlihan

DEDICATION

To family and friends – thanks for all the support over many years. JH

Unlock the secrets to sustainable success with 'Green from Green II – Businesses & Utilities':

This book provides an essential guide that empowers managers to level up their approach to energy consumption, emissions reduction, and efficiency enhancement – it could be considered a manager's playbook of energy transition strategies for the 2020's.

Dive into a comprehensive exploration starting with an introduction to sustainable management, followed by meticulous auditing and analysis of energy consumption.

Discover actionable strategies for reducing emissions and identify key improvement opportunities to enhance efficiency. With guidance from various authorities, including for example the AEE and their comprehensive Certified Energy Management training curriculum, this book offers long-term strategies to sustain green practices.

Equip yourself with the knowledge and tools to lead your organization towards a greener, more sustainable, and more profitable future.

CONTENTS

INTRODUCTION 1

1 INTRODUCTION TO SUSTAINABLE MANAGEMENT 3

1.1 The Green Revolution in Business: Why Sustainability Matters 5
1.2 Defining Sustainable Management Practices 10
1.3 The Transformative Benefits of Implementing Green Strategies 14
1.4 Navigating the Landscape of Environmental Regulations and Compliance 20
1.5 AEE CEM Curriculum: The Bedrock of Sustainable Leadership 24

2 ENERGY CONSUMPTION: AUDITING AND ANALYSIS . 33

2.1 Conducting Comprehensive Energy Audits 36
Pinpointing Energy Hotspots: A Comprehensive Guide 42
2.2 Harnessing the Power of Energy Management Systems (EMS) for Optimal Efficiency 46
2.3 Analyzing Energy Data for Informed Decision-Making 51
2.4 Case Studies - Successful Energy Audits 55
2.5 Real-Life Success Stories in Energy Auditing and Analysis 59

3 REDUCING EMISSIONS: STRATEGIES AND IMPLEMENTATION 64

3.1 Understanding Different Types of Emissions 66
3.2 Setting Emission Reduction Goals: The Blueprint for a Sustainable Future 71
3.3 Implementing Green Technologies and Practices 77
3.4 Emissions Monitoring and Reporting: The Cornerstones of Sustainable Management 83
3.5 Unlocking Financial Support: Government Incentives and Grants for Emission Reduction 89
3.6 Real-Life Success Stories in Emission Reduction 93

4 IMPROVEMENT OPPORTUNITIES: ENHANCING EFFICIENCY 98

4.1 PINPOINTING POTENTIAL: IDENTIFYING AND PRIORITIZING IMPROVEMENT AREAS 100
4.2 ENERGY-EFFICIENT BUILDING DESIGN AND RETROFIT OPTIONS 104
4.3 HARNESSING THE POWER OF THE SUN: SOLAR ENERGY FOR ENHANCED EFFICIENCY 108
4.4 BEHAVIOURAL CHANGES AND EMPLOYEE ENGAGEMENT 114
4.5 QUANTIFYING THE ROI OF SUSTAINABILITY INITIATIVES 118

5 SUSTAINABLE GREEN PRACTICES: LONG-TERM STRATEGIES 123

5.1 CREATING A CULTURE OF SUSTAINABILITY 125
5.2 CONTINUOUS MONITORING AND OPTIMIZATION 128
5.3 TRAINING AND DEVELOPMENT FOR GREEN COMPETENCIES ..132
5.4 BUILDING ROBUST PARTNERSHIPS WITH GREEN ORGANIZATIONS 136
5.5 FUTURE TRENDS IN SUSTAINABLE MANAGEMENT 140

ACKNOWLEDGMENTS

The author wishes to thank any companies, brands and organizations for publishing the materials and success stories on the internet.
These were broadly referred to in the various case studies used in adding colour to this book – without the success stories, it would be very hard to move the rest of the world in the right direction! JH

INTRODUCTION

Imagine a bustling corporate headquarters, where every light, every computer, and every HVAC system hums with activity. The energy bills are sky-high, and the carbon footprint is even more daunting. Now, picture Sarah, a dedicated manager, who decided to transform this energy-guzzling behemoth into a model of sustainability. Her journey wasn't easy, but with the right strategies, tools, and determination, Sarah led her company to a greener, more efficient future. This is the kind of transformation 'Green from Green II - Businesses & Utilities' aims to inspire and guide.

The purpose of this book is to provide managers with the knowledge and strategies needed to transition their organizations towards sustainable practices. As we navigate the complexities of the 2020s, the urgency for sustainable management has never been greater. This book is designed to provide a general guide for the uninitiated, offering practical insights and actionable plans to audit, analyze, and improve your organization's energy consumption and emissions.

Key themes explored in this book include energy auditing, emissions reduction, efficiency enhancement, and long-term sustainability. Each chapter delves into these themes, providing detailed strategies and real-world examples to illustrate their application. From understanding the fundamentals of sustainable management to implementing strategies and improvement opportunities inspired by the AEE Certified Energy Management curriculum, this short book attempts to summarize it for management.

This book is structured to take you on a step-by-step journey beginning with an introduction to sustainable management, setting the stage for deeper dives into more specific areas such as energy consumption auditing, emissions reduction strategies, and efficiency improvement opportunities. The final chapters focus on sustaining green practices over the long term, ensuring that your efforts lead to lasting change.

While this book attempts to offer a comprehensive guide to sustainable business management, it is important to acknowledge its scope and limitations. It focuses primarily on the strategies applicable to corporate and organizational settings, and while the principles can be adapted to other contexts, the specific guidance is tailored for business managers. Additionally, the book emphasizes practical implementation, and while it includes theoretical insights, its primary goal is to provide actionable strategies.

The significance of this 'playbook' lies in its practical approach and its alignment with authoritative cross-industry guidelines such as the AEE and its Certified Energy Management training curriculum. By bridging theory and practice, this book makes a valuable contribution to the field of sustainable management, offering managers the tools they need to lead their organizations towards a greener future.

In summary, this introduction has provided an overview of the book's topic, purpose, and goals. It has identified key themes, discussed the structure and organization, explained the scope and limitations, and highlighted the book's significance. As you turn the pages, you will find a wealth of knowledge and strategies to help you make a meaningful impact on your organization's sustainability journey.

Welcome to 'Green from Green II - Businesses & Utilities'.

1 INTRODUCTION TO SUSTAINABLE MANAGEMENT

Source Pexels - Photo by Tran Le Tuan:

As we navigate the complexities of the 2020s, one principle stands out as both a challenge and an opportunity for businesses across the globe: sustainability. In an era of heightened environmental awareness and unprecedented technological advancements, sustainable management has become crucial to long-term success. 'Green from Green II - Businesses & Utilities' is designed to guide forward-thinking managers through the intricate landscape of sustainability, offering practical insights and actionable strategies to transform their organizations into eco-efficiency models.

The importance of sustainability in business cannot be overstated. As the repercussions of climate change become increasingly evident, consumers, stakeholders, and regulatory bodies are demanding greater accountability and transparency from companies. Sustainable management practices are no longer optional; they are a business imperative. By embracing these practices, companies can not only mitigate their environmental impact but also unlock new avenues for growth, innovation, and competitive advantage.

So, what exactly does sustainable management entail? At its core, sustainable management is about integrating environmental stewardship into every facet of business operations. This means going beyond mere compliance with environmental regulations and striving to minimize resource consumption, reduce waste, and lower emissions. It involves a holistic approach that considers the long-term impacts of business activities on the planet and society, ensuring that economic growth does not come at the expense of environmental degradation.

The benefits of implementing green strategies are manifold. For one, companies that adopt sustainable practices often find themselves more resilient to market fluctuations and regulatory changes. By reducing dependency on finite resources and enhancing energy efficiency, these businesses can achieve cost savings and improve their bottom line. Additionally, sustainability initiatives can enhance brand reputation and customer loyalty, as consumers increasingly prefer to support companies that demonstrate a genuine commitment to environmental responsibility.

Moreover, sustainable management opens the door to innovation. By rethinking traditional processes and exploring new technologies, companies can develop cutting-edge solutions that not only address environmental challenges but also drive business growth. From renewable energy adoption to circular economy models, the possibilities are vast and varied.

However, navigating the path to sustainability requires a thorough understanding of the regulatory landscape. Environmental regulations and compliance standards are continually evolving, and staying abreast of these changes is crucial for businesses aiming to maintain their sustainability credentials. This book provides an overview of the key regulations and compliance requirements that managers need to be aware of, ensuring that they can effectively align their strategies with legal obligations.

To equip managers with the necessary knowledge and skills, 'Green from Green II - Businesses & Utilities' also introduces the AEE Certified Energy Management curriculum. Developed by the Association of Energy Engineers (AEE), this curriculum offers a comprehensive framework for energy management, covering everything from energy auditing and analysis to the implementation of energy-saving measures. By incorporating insights from this respected authority, the book ensures that readers are well-prepared to undertake the journey towards sustainable management.

In this introductory chapter, we will explore the foundational concepts of sustainable management, delving into its significance, defining its practices, and highlighting the numerous benefits it offers. We will also provide an overview of the environmental regulations that shape the sustainable management landscape and introduce the AEE Certified Energy Management curriculum as a valuable resource for managers. By the end of this chapter, readers will have a clear understanding of the importance of sustainability in business and be equipped with the knowledge needed to embark on their own sustainability journey. Welcome to the first step towards a greener, more sustainable future.

1.1 The Green Revolution in Business: Why Sustainability Matters

The Emergence of the Green Economy

In recent years, the landscape of global business has been dramatically transformed by the emergence of the green economy. This shift is not merely a trend or a fad, as some might hope, but rather a fundamental change in how businesses will operate and thrive in the future. The green economy encompasses a wide range of activities, products, and services that are designed with environmental sustainability in mind. Companies across various sectors are recognizing that sustainable practices are not only good for the planet but also beneficial for their bottom line.

The rise of the green economy can be attributed to several key factors:

Firstly, there is an increasing awareness among consumers about the environmental impact of their purchasing decisions. Today's consumers are more informed and conscientious than ever before, and they are demanding products and services that align with their values. This shift in consumer behaviour has created a significant market opportunity for businesses that prioritize sustainability.

Secondly, governments and regulatory bodies around the world are implementing stricter environmental regulations. These regulations are designed to reduce carbon emissions, promote renewable energy, and minimize waste. Businesses that fail to comply with these regulations risk facing substantial fines and reputational damage. On the other hand, companies that proactively adopt sustainable practices can benefit from incentives such as tax breaks and grants.

Finally, the financial sector is increasingly recognizing the importance of sustainability. Investors are looking for companies that demonstrate strong environmental, social, and governance (ESG) performance. Sustainable businesses are often viewed as less risky and more resilient, making them attractive investment opportunities. As a result, companies are under pressure to integrate sustainability into their core strategies to attract and retain investment.

The Triple Bottom Line: People, Planet, Profit

One of the foundational principles of sustainable management is the 'Triple Bottom Line' (TBL), a concept introduced by John Elkington in the mid-1990s and later adopted by Shell – yes, that one – the international oil and gas behemoth! The TBL framework encourages businesses to focus not only on financial performance but also on social and environmental impacts. Achieving a balance between people, planet, and profit ensures that a business can thrive while contributing positively to society and minimizing its ecological footprint.

1. People: A sustainable business prioritizes the well-being of its employees, customers, and communities. This means creating a safe and inclusive workplace, offering fair wages and benefits, and engaging in ethical business practices. By investing in people, businesses can enhance employee satisfaction and productivity, build customer loyalty, and contribute to the social fabric of the communities in which they operate.
2. Planet: Environmental stewardship is a core component of the triple bottom line. Sustainable businesses strive to minimize their ecological footprint by reducing waste, conserving resources, and using renewable energy. This not only helps protect the planet but also reduces operational costs and mitigates risks associated with resource scarcity and environmental degradation.
3. Profit: Financial performance remains a critical aspect of business success. However, the triple bottom line approach recognizes that profitability and sustainability are not mutually exclusive. In fact, sustainable practices can drive innovation, enhance brand reputation, and open up new market opportunities. Companies that integrate sustainability into their business models are often better positioned for long-term growth and profitability.

The Business Case for Sustainability
The business case for sustainability is strong and multifaceted. Companies that adopt sustainable practices can realize numerous benefits, including cost savings, risk mitigation, and enhanced competitiveness.

Cost Savings
One of the most immediate and tangible benefits of sustainability is cost savings. By reducing energy consumption, minimizing waste, and optimizing resource use, businesses can significantly lower their operational expenses. For example, energy-efficient technologies and practices can lead to substantial reductions in utility bills. Similarly, waste reduction initiatives can reduce disposal costs and even generate revenue through recycling and repurposing materials.

Risk Mitigation
Sustainability can also help businesses mitigate a wide range of risks. Environmental risks, such as climate change and resource scarcity, can have profound impacts on business operations and supply chains. By adopting sustainable practices, companies can reduce their vulnerability to these risks. Additionally, sustainability can help businesses navigate regulatory risks by ensuring compliance with environmental laws and standards. This not only prevents costly fines and penalties but also enhances corporate reputation and stakeholder trust.

Enhanced Competitiveness
In today's competitive business environment, sustainability can be a key differentiator. Companies that demonstrate a strong commitment to sustainability can enhance their brand reputation and attract environmentally conscious consumers. Moreover, sustainability can drive innovation by encouraging businesses to develop new products, services, and processes that meet the evolving needs of customers and society. This can open up new market opportunities and create a competitive advantage.

The Role of Leadership in Driving Sustainability
Effective leadership is essential for driving sustainability within an organization. Leaders play a critical role in setting the vision, strategy, and culture for sustainability. They must be able to articulate the business case for sustainability, inspire and engage employees, and ensure that sustainability is integrated into all aspects of the business.

Vision and Strategy
Leaders must develop a clear and compelling vision for sustainability that aligns with the company's overall mission and values. This vision should be supported by a robust sustainability strategy that outlines specific goals, targets, and action plans. The strategy should be based on a thorough understanding of the company's environmental and social impacts, as well as the risks and opportunities associated with sustainability.

Employee Engagement
Engaging employees is crucial for the successful implementation of sustainability initiatives. Leaders must foster a culture of sustainability by encouraging employee participation, providing training and resources, and recognizing and rewarding sustainable behaviours. When employees feel empowered and motivated to contribute to sustainability, they are more likely to take ownership of initiatives and drive positive change.

Integration and Accountability
Sustainability should be integrated into all aspects of the business, from product development and supply chain management to marketing and customer relations. Leaders must ensure that sustainability is embedded in decision-making processes and performance metrics. This requires establishing clear accountability and governance structures, as well as regularly monitoring and reporting on progress.

Sustainability as a Driver of Innovation
Sustainability can be a powerful driver of innovation. By challenging traditional business models and practices, sustainability encourages companies to think creatively and develop new solutions that address environmental and social challenges.

Product and Service Innovation
Sustainable innovation often involves the development of new products and services that meet the needs of environmentally conscious consumers. This can include designing products with lower environmental impacts, using sustainable materials, or offering services that promote resource efficiency. For example, companies in the fashion industry are exploring sustainable fabrics and circular business models that reduce waste and extend the lifecycle of products.

Process Innovation
Sustainability can also drive process innovation by encouraging businesses to

optimize their operations and supply chains. This can involve adopting energy-efficient technologies, implementing waste reduction practices, or developing closed-loop systems that minimize resource use and waste generation. Process innovation can lead to significant cost savings and operational efficiencies, as well as reduced environmental impacts.

Business Model Innovation
In some cases, sustainability can lead to entirely new business models that create value for both the company and society. For example, the sharing economy and circular economy are based on principles of sustainability and resource efficiency. These business models prioritize access over ownership, promote the reuse and recycling of materials, and create new opportunities for value creation.

The Future of Sustainable Business
The future of sustainable business is bright, with increasing recognition of the importance of sustainability and growing momentum for change. As businesses continue to embrace sustainable practices, they will play a critical role in addressing global challenges such as climate change, resource scarcity, and social inequality.

Collaborative Partnerships
Collaboration will be key to driving sustainability at scale. Businesses must work together, as well as with governments, non-profit organizations, and other stakeholders, to develop and implement solutions that address systemic challenges. Collaborative partnerships can facilitate knowledge sharing, leverage resources, and create synergies that drive positive change.

Technological Advancements
Technological advancements will also play a crucial role in advancing sustainability. Innovations in areas such as renewable energy, energy storage, and digital technologies have the potential to transform how businesses operate and reduce their environmental impacts. By staying at the forefront of technological developments, companies can enhance their sustainability performance and remain competitive in a rapidly changing world.

Evolving Consumer Expectations
As consumer expectations continue to evolve, businesses must remain responsive and adaptable. Consumers are increasingly looking for transparency and accountability from the companies they support. By demonstrating a genuine commitment to sustainability and engaging with

consumers in meaningful ways, businesses can build trust and loyalty.

Understanding the importance of sustainability in business is essential for managers and leaders who aim to navigate the complexities of the 2020s. By embracing sustainability, businesses can unlock new opportunities, drive innovation, and create lasting value for their stakeholders. The journey towards sustainability requires vision, commitment, and collaboration, but the rewards are significant. As we move forward, sustainable business practices will become the norm rather than the exception, paving the way for a greener, more prosperous future.

1.2 Defining Sustainable Management Practices

In the rapidly evolving corporate landscape of the 2020s, sustainable management is no longer a fringe concept; it is a fundamental pillar for success. Sustainable management practices revolve around the integration of environmental, social, and economic considerations into business operations and decision-making processes. The core idea is to strike a balance between meeting the needs of the present without compromising the ability of future generations to meet their own needs.

This section unpacks the essence of sustainable management practices and explores why they are critical for modern businesses. We also note that the Three P's of the Triple Bottom Line have in reality become the Four P's – People, Planet, Profit, and *Promotion* in the sense of Marketing which must be paramount for any business – after all, "nothing happens until something get's sold" – unfortunately I don't know who to credit for this gem of wisdom - JH.

The Evolution of Corporate Responsibility
Corporate responsibility has evolved significantly over the decades. What began as philanthropic efforts and compliance with regulations has now transformed into a comprehensive approach that integrates sustainability into the core business strategy. This evolution can be traced through several stages:

- Philanthropy and Compliance In the early stages, corporate responsibility was often equated with charitable donations and adherence to environmental regulations. Companies engaged in philanthropy to enhance their public image and mitigate any negative impacts of their operations.

- Strategic CSR As awareness of environmental and social issues grew, businesses began to adopt Corporate Social Responsibility (CSR) strategies that aligned with their core values and operations. This stage saw the integration of CSR into business strategy, with a focus on creating shared value for both the company and society.
- Sustainable Management The current stage transcends traditional CSR by embedding sustainability into every aspect of business operations. It involves proactive measures to create a positive impact on the environment and society while ensuring economic success. Companies are now expected to demonstrate transparency, accountability, and long-term commitment to sustainability.

Key Components of Sustainable Management Practices

To effectively implement sustainable management, businesses must focus on several key components. These components serve as the building blocks for creating a sustainable and resilient organization.

1. Leadership and Governance: Strong leadership is essential for driving sustainability initiatives. Leadership commitment to sustainability must be reflected in the company's vision, mission, and values. Governance structures should include sustainability committees and designated roles to oversee and drive sustainability efforts.
2. Stakeholder Engagement: Engaging with stakeholders—including employees, customers, suppliers, investors, and communities—is critical for understanding their needs and expectations. Open and transparent communication builds trust and fosters collaborative efforts towards sustainability goals.
3. Sustainability Reporting and Transparency: Regular reporting on sustainability performance is vital for accountability and continuous improvement. Companies should adopt recognized frameworks such as the Global Reporting Initiative (GRI) or the Sustainability Accounting Standards Board (SASB) to disclose their environmental, social, and governance (ESG) metrics.
4. Risk Management: Identifying and managing sustainability-related risks—such as climate change, resource scarcity, and regulatory changes—is crucial for long-term resilience. Integrating sustainability into risk management processes helps businesses anticipate and mitigate potential challenges.
5. Innovation and Technology: Leveraging innovation and technology can

drive sustainable solutions. This includes investing in research and development for eco-friendly products, adopting clean technologies, and utilizing digital tools for efficient resource management.

Case Studies: Leading by Example

To illustrate the practical application of sustainable management practices, let's examine a few case studies of companies that have successfully integrated sustainability into their operations.

Patagonia:
Patagonia, an outdoor apparel company, is renowned for its commitment to environmental sustainability. The company's mission statement, "We're in business to save our home planet," reflects its dedication to minimizing its ecological footprint. Patagonia has implemented various initiatives, such as using recycled materials, supporting environmental activism, and promoting fair labour practices.

Unilever:
Unilever, a global consumer goods company, has made significant strides in sustainability through its Sustainable Living Plan. The plan aims to decouple the company's growth from its environmental impact and increase its positive social impact. Unilever focuses on sustainable sourcing, reducing greenhouse gas emissions, and improving health and well-being for over a billion people.

Tesla:
Tesla's mission to accelerate the world's transition to sustainable energy is at the core of its business strategy. The company's innovations in electric vehicles, energy storage, and solar technology exemplify how businesses can drive sustainability through technological advancements. Tesla's commitment to sustainability extends to its supply chain, where it seeks to source materials responsibly and minimize its environmental impact.

Challenges and Overcoming Barriers

While the benefits of sustainable management are clear, businesses may encounter challenges in implementing these practices. Understanding these challenges and developing strategies to overcome them is essential for successful integration.

1. Initial Costs: Implementing sustainable practices may require upfront investments in technology, infrastructure, and training. To overcome this barrier, businesses can seek funding opportunities, such as grants and

incentives, and focus on the long-term financial benefits of sustainability.
2. Cultural Resistance: Shifting to a sustainability-focused mindset may face resistance from employees and stakeholders who are accustomed to traditional practices. Effective change management, including clear communication, education, and involving employees in sustainability initiatives, can help overcome this resistance.
3. Complexity of Measurement: Measuring and reporting on sustainability performance can be complex due to the lack of standardized metrics and the need for comprehensive data collection. Adopting recognized reporting frameworks and leveraging technology for data management can streamline this process.
4. Regulatory Uncertainty: Changes in regulations and policies related to sustainability can create uncertainty for businesses. Staying informed about regulatory developments and engaging in advocacy can help businesses navigate this challenge.
5. Global Supply Chain: Managing sustainability across a global supply chain can be challenging due to varying standards and practices. Collaborating with suppliers, setting clear expectations, and conducting regular audits can ensure consistency in sustainability efforts.

The Future of Sustainable Management

The future of sustainable management is promising, with increasing awareness and commitment from businesses, governments, and consumers. Several trends are shaping the future landscape of sustainable management:

- Circular Economy: The shift towards a circular economy, where products and materials are reused, repaired, and recycled, is gaining momentum. Businesses are exploring innovative ways to design out waste and keep resources in use for as long as possible.
- Climate Action: With the growing urgency to address climate change, businesses are setting ambitious targets for reducing greenhouse gas emissions and transitioning to renewable energy sources. Climate action is becoming a central focus of sustainability strategies.
- Social Responsibility: The emphasis on social responsibility is increasing, with businesses taking a more active role in addressing social issues such as inequality, human rights, and community development. This holistic approach to sustainability is essential for creating a positive societal impact.
- Technological Advancements: Advancements in technology, such as

artificial intelligence, blockchain, and the Internet of Things (IoT), are enabling more efficient and effective sustainability solutions. These technologies can enhance data collection, monitoring, and reporting, driving continuous improvement in sustainability performance.
- Collaborative Efforts: Collaboration and partnerships are becoming crucial for achieving sustainability goals. Businesses are working together with governments, non-profits, and other stakeholders to tackle complex sustainability challenges and drive systemic change.

Defining sustainable management practices is the first step towards creating a sustainable future for businesses and society. By understanding the principles of the Triple Bottom Line, recognizing the evolution of corporate responsibility, and focusing on key components of sustainable management, businesses can drive positive environmental, social, and economic outcomes.

The benefits of sustainable management extend beyond immediate financial gains to include long-term resilience, competitive advantage, and enhanced reputation. While challenges exist, they can be overcome with strategic planning, innovation, and collaboration. As we move forward into the 2020s and beyond, sustainable management will continue to be a critical driver of success for businesses committed to making a positive impact on the world.

1.3 The Transformative Benefits of Implementing Green Strategies

In the modern business landscape, the adoption of green strategies goes beyond mere compliance with regulatory standards. Companies increasingly recognize the transformative benefits that these practices offer across three critical dimensions: people, planet, and profit. This holistic approach provides a comprehensive framework that can drive sustainable success.

People: Enhancing Employee Well-being and Community Relations

One of the most immediate and impactful benefits of implementing green strategies is the positive effect on people—both within and outside the organization. Sustainable practices can significantly enhance employee well-being, which in turn boosts productivity and morale. For instance, companies that invest in energy-efficient lighting and HVAC systems create more comfortable and healthier work environments. This leads to reduced absenteeism and higher employee satisfaction.

Moreover, green strategies often involve community engagement and social responsibility initiatives. By participating in local environmental projects or supporting sustainable development in underserved areas, companies can build stronger relationships with the communities they operate in. This not only enhances the company's reputation but also fosters a sense of purpose among employees, making them feel more connected to their work and their employer.

Planet: Reducing Environmental Impact and Promoting Sustainability

At its core, the implementation of green strategies aims to mitigate the negative environmental impact of business operations. This includes reducing greenhouse gas emissions, minimizing waste, and conserving natural resources. For example, by conducting thorough energy audits and implementing energy-saving measures, companies can significantly decrease their carbon footprint. This not only contributes to global efforts to combat climate change but also aligns the company with increasingly stringent environmental regulations.

In addition to direct environmental benefits, green strategies can also promote sustainability in the supply chain. Companies that prioritize sustainable sourcing and production practices encourage their suppliers to adopt similar measures, creating a ripple effect that extends the positive impact beyond the organization's immediate operations. This holistic approach to sustainability helps build a more resilient and sustainable economy.

Profit: Enhancing Financial Performance and Competitive Advantage

While the environmental and social benefits of green strategies are well-documented, their financial advantages are equally compelling. Implementing energy-efficient technologies and practices can lead to substantial cost savings on utilities and operational expenses. For instance, companies that invest in renewable energy sources such as solar or wind power can reduce their reliance on non-renewable energy and lower their energy bills in the long run.

Moreover, green strategies can enhance a company's competitive advantage. As consumers become more environmentally conscious, they increasingly prefer to do business with companies that demonstrate a commitment to sustainability. By positioning themselves as leaders in environmental stewardship, companies can attract a loyal customer base and differentiate themselves from competitors. Additionally, investors are increasingly favoring companies with strong environmental, social, and governance (ESG) performance, which can lead to greater access to capital and more favourable financing terms.

Operational Efficiency and Innovation

Green strategies often drive operational efficiency and innovation. By adopting sustainable practices, companies are encouraged to rethink their processes and identify areas for improvement. This can lead to the development of innovative solutions that not only reduce environmental impact but also enhance operational performance.

Energy Management and Efficiency

One of the key areas where green strategies can drive efficiency is energy management. By conducting detailed energy audits and implementing advanced energy management systems, companies can identify and eliminate energy wastage. This not only reduces costs but also enhances the overall efficiency of operations. For example, smart building technologies that optimize heating, cooling, and lighting can lead to significant energy savings while maintaining optimal working conditions.

Waste Reduction and Resource Optimization

Another critical aspect of green strategies is waste reduction and resource optimization. By adopting practices such as recycling, composting, and reusing materials, companies can minimize their waste output and reduce the environmental impact of their operations. Additionally, optimizing resource use—such as water and raw materials—can lead to cost savings and more sustainable production processes. For instance, companies in the manufacturing sector can implement lean manufacturing principles to reduce material waste and improve resource efficiency.

Product and Process Innovation

The pursuit of sustainability often drives innovation in product design and manufacturing processes. Companies that prioritize green strategies are more likely to develop new products that are environmentally friendly and meet the growing demand for sustainable alternatives. For example, the development of biodegradable packaging materials or energy-efficient appliances not only addresses environmental concerns but also opens up new market opportunities.

Regulatory Compliance and Risk Management

In an era of increasing environmental regulations and stakeholder expectations, green strategies play a crucial role in ensuring regulatory compliance and managing risks. Companies that proactively adopt sustainable practices are better positioned to navigate the complex regulatory landscape and avoid potential legal and financial penalties.

Adherence to Environmental Regulations

Governments and regulatory bodies worldwide are implementing stricter environmental regulations to address the pressing issues of climate change, pollution, and resource depletion. By staying ahead of these regulations and formally adopting green strategies, companies can ensure compliance and avoid costly fines or shutdowns. For instance, implementing emissions reduction measures and monitoring systems can help companies meet air quality standards and reduce their environmental footprint.

Risk Mitigation and Resilience

Green strategies also contribute to risk mitigation and resilience. Companies that prioritize sustainability are better equipped to manage environmental risks, such as natural disasters, resource scarcity, and supply chain disruptions. For example, by diversifying energy sources and investing in renewable energy, companies can reduce their vulnerability to fluctuations in energy prices and supply shortages. Additionally, sustainable practices such as water conservation and waste management can enhance the resilience of operations in the face of environmental challenges.

Promotion: Brand, HR, Employee Engagement and Talent Attraction

Implementing green strategies can have a profound impact on employee engagement and talent attraction. In today's competitive job market, employees increasingly seek employers that align with their values and prioritize sustainability. By demonstrating a commitment to environmental stewardship, companies can attract and retain top talent, fostering a motivated and engaged workforce.

Creating a Purpose-Driven Culture

Green strategies can help create a purpose-driven culture within the organization. When employees see that their company is actively working towards reducing its environmental impact and contributing to a sustainable future, they are more likely to feel a sense of pride and purpose in their work.

This can lead to higher levels of engagement, job satisfaction, and loyalty. Moreover, companies that involve employees in sustainability initiatives, such as green teams or volunteer programs, can further strengthen their commitment to the organization's sustainability goals.

Attracting Environmentally Conscious Talent
As the workforce becomes increasingly environmentally conscious, companies that prioritize sustainability have a competitive edge in attracting top talent. Job seekers, particularly millennials and Gen Z, are more likely to choose employers that demonstrate a commitment to social and environmental responsibility. By showcasing their green strategies and sustainability achievements, companies can appeal to these environmentally conscious candidates and build a diverse and talented workforce.

Brand Reputation and Market Positioning
In the age of information and social media, a company's brand reputation is more important than ever. Implementing green strategies can significantly enhance a company's reputation and market positioning, leading to increased brand loyalty and customer trust.

Building a Positive Brand Image
Green strategies contribute to building a positive brand image by demonstrating a company's commitment to sustainability and social responsibility. Consumers are more likely to support and trust brands that align with their values and take meaningful actions to protect the environment. By showcasing their green initiatives through marketing campaigns, sustainability reports, and social media, companies can enhance their brand reputation and differentiate themselves in the market.

Gaining a Competitive Edge
In an increasingly competitive marketplace, green strategies can provide a significant competitive edge. Companies that prioritize sustainability and environmental stewardship can attract environmentally conscious customers who are willing to pay a premium for sustainable products and services. This can lead to increased market share and revenue growth. Additionally, companies that integrate sustainability into their core business strategy are better positioned to respond to changing market trends and customer preferences, ensuring long-term success.

Conclusion: A Holistic Approach to Success
The transformative benefits of implementing green strategies extend far

beyond regulatory compliance and cost savings. By adopting a holistic approach that considers the triple bottom line—people, planet, and profit—companies can drive sustainable success and create lasting value. From enhancing employee well-being and community relations to reducing environmental impact and promoting innovation, green strategies offer a wide range of benefits that can significantly impact a company's performance and reputation.

As we navigate the challenges and opportunities of the 2020s, the importance of sustainable management cannot be overstated. Companies that embrace green strategies and prioritize sustainability are better equipped to thrive in a rapidly changing business landscape. By leveraging the insights and strategies outlined in 'Green from Green II - Businesses & Utilities', managers can lead their organizations towards a greener, more sustainable future, unlocking the full potential of sustainable success.

1.4 Navigating the Landscape of Environmental Regulations and Compliance

In today's increasingly eco-conscious world, the role of a green manager requires a nuanced understanding of environmental regulations and compliance. These regulations serve as the bedrock upon which sustainable practices are built, guiding organizations in their quest for efficiency, reduced emissions, and overall environmental stewardship.

This section discusses the complexities of environmental regulations and compliance, providing a comprehensive overview to help green managers navigate this critical aspect of sustainable management.

The Evolution of Environmental Regulations

Historical Context
The inception of environmental regulations can be traced back to the early 20th century when industrialization began to take a noticeable toll on the environment. The initial focus was on public health concerns related to air and water quality. Over time, as scientific understanding of environmental issues deepened, regulations evolved to address a broader spectrum of concerns, including waste management, greenhouse gas emissions, and biodiversity conservation.

Key Milestones
- The Clean Air Act (1963): One of the earliest and most influential pieces

of environmental legislation in the United States, aimed at controlling air pollution on a national level.
- The Clean Water Act (1972): This act established the basic structure for regulating pollutant discharges into U.S. waters and quality standards for surface waters.
- The Kyoto Protocol (1997): An international treaty that committed its parties to reduce greenhouse gas emissions, based on the premise that global warming exists and is human-caused.
- The Paris Agreement (2015): A landmark international accord that brought all nations into a common cause to undertake ambitious efforts to combat climate change and adapt to its effects.

The Regulatory Framework: National vs. International Regulations
Environmental regulations exist at both national and international levels, each with its own set of requirements, enforcement mechanisms, and compliance strategies. US national regulations are typically enforced by governmental bodies such as the Environmental Protection Agency (EPA) in the United States, while international regulations are overseen by organizations like the United Nations and the European Union.

Key Regulatory Bodies
- Environmental Protection Agency (EPA): Responsible for the protection of human health and the environment in the United States.
- European Environment Agency (EEA): Provides sound, independent information on the environment to those involved in developing, adopting, implementing, and evaluating environmental policy, and also to the general public.
- United Nations Environment Programme (UNEP): The leading global environmental authority that sets the global environmental agenda, promotes the coherent implementation of the environmental dimension of sustainable development within the United Nations system, and serves as an authoritative advocate for the global environment.

Compliance Strategies for Greener Management
Risk Assessment and Management
Effective compliance begins with a thorough risk assessment to identify potential environmental impacts and regulatory requirements specific to the organization's operations. This involves:

- Identifying Risks: Catalogue all activities that might have environmental impacts, such as emissions, waste generation, and resource consumption.
- Evaluating Risks: Assessing the severity and likelihood of each identified risk including risks associated with production losses.
- Mitigating Risks: Implementing measures to minimize or eliminate identified risks, including technological upgrades, process changes, and employee training.

Environmental Management Systems (EMS)
An Environmental Management System (EMS) is a structured framework that helps an organization achieve its environmental goals through consistent review, evaluation, and improvement of its environmental performance. Key components include:

- Policy Development: Establishing an environmental policy that outlines the organization's commitment to compliance and sustainability.
- Planning: Identifying environmental aspects and impacts, legal requirements, and objectives and targets for improvement.
- Implementation and Operation: Defining roles and responsibilities, training employees, and establishing communication channels.
- Checking and Corrective Action: Monitoring and measuring environmental performance, conducting audits, and taking corrective actions as necessary.
- Management Review: Periodically reviewing the EMS to ensure its continued suitability, adequacy, and effectiveness.

Case Studies in Compliance

Case Study 1: XYZ Manufacturing
Background: XYZ Manufacturing, a mid-sized company in the automotive sector, faced significant challenges in meeting the stringent emissions standards set by both national and international regulators.

Approach: The company implemented a comprehensive EMS, focusing on reducing emissions through technological upgrades and process optimization. They also invested in employee training to ensure adherence to new protocols.

Outcome: XYZ Manufacturing not only achieved compliance but also realized cost savings through improved efficiency and reduced waste. Their proactive approach earned them recognition from industry peers and regulatory bodies.

Case Study 2: ABC Energy
Background: ABC Energy, a large multinational corporation, was struggling with compliance across its diverse operations in multiple countries, each with its own set of regulations.

Approach: ABC Energy established a global compliance team to oversee regulatory requirements and implemented a centralized EMS to standardize processes across all locations. They also leveraged technology for real-time monitoring and reporting.

Outcome: The company successfully harmonized its compliance efforts, resulting in improved environmental performance and a stronger reputation in the global market.

The Role of Technology in Compliance
Monitoring and Reporting
Advancements in technology have revolutionized the way organizations monitor and report their environmental impact. Modern tools and software solutions can track emissions, resource consumption, and waste generation in real-time, providing valuable data for compliance and continuous improvement.

Automation and AI
Automation and Artificial Intelligence (AI) are playing increasingly significant roles in environmental compliance. Automated systems can handle routine compliance tasks, such as data collection and reporting, while AI can analyze large datasets to identify trends, predict potential issues, and recommend corrective actions.

The Future of Environmental Regulations
Emerging Trends
As the global focus on sustainability intensifies, several emerging trends are likely to shape the future of environmental regulations:

Climate Change Legislation: New laws aimed at mitigating climate change are expected to become more stringent, with an emphasis on reducing carbon footprints and promoting renewable energy.

Circular Economy: Regulations promoting the circular economy, which focuses on minimizing waste and maximizing resource efficiency, are gaining traction worldwide.

Corporate Transparency: There is a growing demand for greater transparency and accountability in corporate environmental practices, leading to more rigorous reporting requirements.

Preparing for the Future
Green managers must stay abreast of these emerging trends and proactively adapt their strategies to remain compliant. This involves continuous learning, staying informed about legislative changes, and fostering a culture of sustainability within the organization.

Navigating the complex landscape of environmental regulations and compliance is a critical responsibility for green managers. By understanding the historical context, regulatory framework, compliance strategies, and emerging trends, managers can effectively guide their organizations toward sustainable success. The journey requires a proactive approach, leveraging technology and fostering a culture of continuous improvement. As regulations evolve, green managers must remain vigilant, adaptable, and committed to the overarching goal of environmental stewardship.

1.5 AEE CEM Curriculum: The Bedrock of Sustainable Leadership

The Association of Energy Engineers (AEE) Certified Energy Management (CEM) curriculum is one but not the only cornerstone in the realm of sustainable management. There are many national organisations but one will find that the AEE and the ISO standards, more specifically ISO50000, will inform many of the approaches to audit that are outlined here.

For any manager looking to navigate the complexities of energy consumption, emissions reduction, and efficiency improvement, understanding and integrating the principles taught in this curriculum is not just recommended but essential.

This section looks into the AEE CEM curriculum, elucidating its relevance, core components, and practical applications in the journey towards sustainable management.

What Is & Why An AEE CEM Approach?
The value proposition of the AEE CEM curriculum is globally recognized for its comprehensive approach to energy management. It is designed to equip professionals with the knowledge and skills necessary to optimize energy

usage and implement sustainable practices within their organizations. The curriculum's value proposition lies in its holistic approach, covering everything from energy auditing and analysis to advanced strategies for emissions reduction and efficiency enhancement.

By adhering to the AEE CEM guidelines, managers can ensure their practices are aligned with international standards and best practices, thereby driving their organizations towards a greener future.

Core Components of the AEE CEM Curriculum

The AEE CEM curriculum is structured around several key components, each designed to build a robust foundation in energy management. These components include:

1. Energy Auditing and Analysis: This module emphasizes the importance of conducting thorough energy audits to identify areas of inefficiency and potential improvement. It covers various auditing techniques, tools, and methodologies that help in accurately assessing energy consumption patterns.
2. Energy Accounting and Economics: Understanding the economic implications of energy consumption is crucial for any sustainable management strategy. This component delves into energy accounting principles, cost-benefit analysis, and financial metrics that are essential for making informed decisions.
3. Energy Management Systems (EnMS): Implementing an effective EnMS is pivotal for continuous improvement in energy performance. This module outlines the structure and requirements of an EnMS, including the ISO 50001 standard, which provides a framework for establishing, implementing, maintaining, and improving energy management.
4. Energy Efficiency and Renewable Energy: The curriculum explores various strategies for enhancing energy efficiency and integrating renewable energy sources. It covers topics such as energy-efficient technologies, demand-side management, and the benefits of renewable energy adoption.
5. Sustainability and Environmental Impact: This component focuses on the broader environmental implications of energy consumption. It addresses strategies for reducing carbon footprints, managing emissions, and promoting sustainability within organizational practices.

Practical Applications: Bringing Theory to Practice
One of the standout features of the AEE CEM curriculum is its emphasis on practical applications. The curriculum is designed not just to impart theoretical knowledge but to equip managers with actionable insights and tools that can be implemented in real-world scenarios. Here we explore how these core components translate into practical strategies for sustainable management.

Conducting Effective Energy Audits
Energy audits are the starting point for any energy management initiative. The AEE CEM curriculum provides a detailed roadmap for conducting these audits, from preliminary assessments to detailed evaluations. Managers are trained to use specialized tools and techniques to gather data, analyse energy consumption patterns, and identify inefficiencies.

For instance, a facility manager might use the guidelines from the curriculum to conduct a comprehensive energy audit of a manufacturing plant. By examining energy usage across different processes and equipment, the manager can pinpoint areas where energy is being wasted and recommend changes such as upgrading to energy-efficient machinery or optimizing production schedules to reduce peak demand.

Integrating Energy Accounting and Economics
The financial aspect of energy management cannot be overstated. The AEE CEM curriculum teaches managers to perform cost-benefit analyses and understand the economic impact of their energy management decisions. This knowledge is crucial for securing buy-in from stakeholders and justifying investments in energy-saving initiatives. Consider a scenario where a manager is proposing the installation of solar panels at a corporate office. By leveraging the principles of energy accounting and economics, the manager can present a compelling case that highlights the long-term cost savings, potential tax incentives, and the positive impact on the company's sustainability goals.

Implementing Energy Management Systems (EnMS)
Establishing an EnMS is a strategic move for organizations committed to continuous improvement in energy performance. The AEE CEM curriculum provides a step-by-step guide to implementing an EnMS, including the development of energy policies, setting performance targets, and conducting regular reviews.

The definition given by the United Nations is as follows:

"An energy management system [...] is a framework for energy consumers, including industrial, commercial and public sector organizations, to manage their energy use. It helps companies identify opportunities to adopt and improve energy-saving technologies, including those that do not necessarily require high capital investment. In most cases, the successful implementation of an EnMS requires specialized expertise and staff training."

All organisations need to be more competitive – this is more or less "a given". A part of this is using resources efficiently – lower costs can mean higher profits or, at the very least, more effective product or service delivery. However, energy management is as much about preventing pollution as conserving resources.

A practical example would be a manager at a hospital who wants to implement an ISO 50001-compliant EnMS. By following the curriculum's guidelines, the manager can develop a comprehensive energy management plan that includes monitoring energy use in various departments, setting reduction targets, and engaging staff in energy-saving practices. The result is a more energy-efficient hospital that not only reduces operational costs but also enhances patient care by ensuring a reliable energy supply.

Enhancing Energy Efficiency and Adopting Renewable Energy
The curriculum's focus on energy efficiency and renewable energy is particularly relevant in today's context of rising energy costs and growing environmental concerns. Managers are trained to identify opportunities for enhancing energy efficiency, such as upgrading lighting systems, improving HVAC operations, and implementing advanced control systems.

For example, a manager at a logistics company might use the curriculum's insights to implement energy-efficient lighting in warehouses and optimize route planning to reduce fuel consumption. Additionally, by exploring renewable energy options, the manager could propose the installation of wind turbines at distribution centres, thereby further reducing the company's carbon footprint and energy costs.

Promoting Sustainability and Managing Environmental Impact
The AEE CEM curriculum's emphasis on sustainability and environmental impact management aligns with the growing demand for corporate social responsibility. Managers are equipped with strategies to reduce emissions, manage waste, and promote sustainable practices throughout their

organizations.

Take the case of a manager at a food processing company who wants to minimize the environmental impact of production processes. By applying the curriculum's principles, the manager can develop a comprehensive sustainability plan that includes measures such as reducing water usage, optimizing supply chains to minimize transportation emissions, and implementing recycling programs for waste materials.

Conclusion: Empowering Sustainable Leaders

In conclusion, the AEE Certified Energy Management curriculum is an invaluable resource for managers seeking to lead their organizations towards a sustainable future. Its comprehensive approach, combining theoretical knowledge with practical applications, empowers managers to make informed decisions, implement effective energy management strategies, and promote sustainability within their organizations.

By integrating the principles of the AEE CEM curriculum into their management practices, managers can not only achieve significant energy savings and reduce environmental impact but also position their organizations as leaders in the realm of sustainable management. The journey towards a greener future begins with education, and the AEE CEM curriculum provides the essential knowledge and tools to embark on this transformative path.

Examples : Real-Life Success Stories in Sustainable Management

To truly understand the impact and potential of sustainable management, it is essential to look at real-life examples of organizations and individuals who have successfully implemented green strategies. These stories not only provide inspiration but also offer practical insights into the challenges and triumphs faced along the way. Below are three detailed case studies that highlight the importance and benefits of sustainable management practices.

<u>Turning A New Leaf: How a Paper Company Became a Sustainability Pioneer</u>
In the early 2000s, Greenleaf Paper Company was facing significant challenges. Known for its high-quality paper products, the company was also notorious for its substantial environmental footprint. The production process was resource-intensive, resulting in high energy consumption, significant emissions, and considerable waste. The leadership team recognized that continuing on this path was unsustainable, both environmentally and economically.

Determined to make a change, Greenleaf Paper Company embarked on a comprehensive sustainability initiative. They started by conducting a thorough energy audit, guided by the principles outlined in the AEE CEM curriculum. This audit revealed several areas of inefficiency, from outdated machinery to energy-intensive lighting systems.

Armed with this information, the company set ambitious goals to reduce energy consumption and emissions. They invested in modern, energy-efficient machinery, which not only reduced energy usage but also improved production efficiency. Additionally, they upgraded their lighting systems to LED technology, significantly lowering electricity consumption.

But Greenleaf didn't stop there. They also implemented a robust recycling program, reducing waste and promoting the use of recycled materials in their products. The company worked closely with environmental regulators to ensure compliance with all relevant regulations, setting a new industry standard for sustainability.

The results were astounding. Within five years, Greenleaf Paper Company reduced its energy consumption by 40%, cut emissions by 35%, and decreased waste by 50%. These improvements not only benefited the environment but also led to substantial cost savings, enhancing the company's bottom line. Today, Greenleaf is celebrated as a pioneer in sustainable management, demonstrating that businesses can thrive while prioritizing the planet.

Green Revolution: The Transformation of an Urban Hotel
The Grand City Hotel was a historic landmark in the heart of a bustling metropolis. While it offered luxury accommodations and top-notch service, it also faced criticism for its environmental impact. The hotel's energy consumption was sky-high, and its waste management practices were outdated. Recognizing the need for change, the hotel's management decided to embark on a journey toward sustainability.

The first step was to conduct a comprehensive energy audit. Partnering with experts from the AEE Certified Energy Management curriculum, the hotel identified several key areas for improvement. The audit revealed that the hotel's HVAC system was a major energy drain, and its lighting and water heating systems were equally inefficient.

To address these issues, the Grand City Hotel implemented a series of green strategies. They upgraded the HVAC system to a state-of-the-art, energy-efficient model, significantly reducing energy consumption. The hotel also replaced all incandescent bulbs with LED lighting, slashing electricity usage. Water conservation was another critical focus. The hotel installed low-flow faucets and showerheads, reducing water consumption without compromising guest comfort. They also introduced a linen reuse program, encouraging guests to opt out of daily towel and sheet changes to save water and energy. The hotel's commitment to sustainability extended beyond energy and water usage. They implemented a comprehensive recycling program and sourced eco-friendly products for their guest amenities. The management team also engaged staff in sustainability training, fostering a culture of environmental responsibility. The transformation was remarkable.

Within three years, the Grand City Hotel reduced its energy consumption by 30%, cut water usage by 25%, and significantly decreased waste. These efforts not only enhanced the hotel's reputation but also attracted a new wave of eco-conscious travellers, boosting occupancy rates and revenue. The Grand City Hotel's green revolution serves as a shining example of how sustainable management can drive both environmental and economic success.

Greening the Supply Chain: A Tech Giant's Commitment to Sustainability
In the competitive world of technology, companies are constantly seeking ways to innovate and stay ahead of the curve.

For TechWorld Inc., a leading global tech company, this meant not only advancing their products but also their sustainability practices. The company recognized that to truly make a difference, it needed to address the environmental impact of its entire supply chain. TechWorld began by conducting a thorough audit of its supply chain. This audit revealed several areas where improvements could be made, from energy-intensive manufacturing processes to inefficient transportation methods.

One of the first steps TechWorld took was to partner with their suppliers to implement energy-saving measures. They worked closely with manufacturers to upgrade to energy-efficient machinery and adopt renewable energy sources. This not only reduced the carbon footprint of their production processes but also resulted in cost savings for their suppliers.

Transportation was another critical focus area. TechWorld optimized their logistics network to reduce fuel consumption and emissions. They introduced more efficient routing and invested in a fleet of hybrid and electric delivery vehicles. Additionally, the company explored opportunities for local sourcing, reducing the need for long-distance transportation and further cutting emissions. TechWorld's commitment to sustainability extended to their product design as well. They prioritized the use of eco-friendly materials and implemented recycling programs for their electronic products. The company also set ambitious goals for reducing packaging waste, opting for recyclable and biodegradable materials.

The results of these efforts were substantial. TechWorld achieved a 25% reduction in supply chain emissions within three years, significantly lowering its overall environmental impact. These achievements not only enhanced the company's reputation as a sustainability leader but also resonated with consumers, who increasingly prioritize eco-friendly products. TechWorld's holistic approach to greening its supply chain demonstrates the power of sustainable management practices. By addressing every aspect of their operations, the company not only improved their environmental performance but also strengthened their competitive advantage in the tech industry.

Conclusion: The Foundation of Sustainable Management

As we conclude this introductory chapter, it's clear that sustainability is not just a buzzword but a critical imperative for modern businesses. Understanding the importance of sustainability in business reveals that it fosters long-term profitability, improves brand reputation, and ensures operational resilience.

By defining sustainable management practices, we've established a framework that integrates environmental, social, and economic considerations into business strategies.

The key benefits of implementing green strategies are manifold, including cost savings, regulatory compliance, and enhanced stakeholder engagement. Moreover, a solid grasp of environmental regulations and compliance is essential for avoiding legal pitfalls and achieving sustainability goals.

Lastly, the introduction to the AEE Certified Energy Management Curriculum provides a structured path for professionals to gain expertise in energy management, driving further efficiencies and innovations.

Key Takeaways:
1. Embrace sustainability as a core business strategy to ensure long-term success and resilience.
2. Implement defined sustainable management practices to integrate environmental, social, and economic goals.
3. Recognize the multifaceted benefits of green strategies, from cost savings to improved stakeholder relations.
4. Stay informed and compliant with environmental regulations to mitigate risks and capitalize on opportunities.
5. Invest in professional development, such as the AEE Certified Energy Management Curriculum, to lead your organization in energy efficiency and sustainable innovation.

6.

Actionable Advice:
1. Begin with a sustainability audit to identify areas for improvement within your organization.
2. Develop a comprehensive sustainability plan that includes clear goals, initiatives, and metrics for success.
3. Engage stakeholders at all levels to foster a culture of sustainability and drive collective action.
4. Regularly review and update your practices to stay aligned with evolving regulations and industry best practices.
5. Seek out certification and training programs to enhance your team's expertise and commitment to sustainable management.

By embedding these principles and actions into your business operations, you will be well-equipped to navigate the challenges and seize the opportunities of the 2020s and beyond.

Welcome to the journey of sustainable management.

2 ENERGY CONSUMPTION: AUDITING AND ANALYSIS

Source: Pexels - Photo by Artem Saranin:

In the quest for a sustainable future, understanding and managing energy consumption stands as one of the most critical challenges—and opportunities—for modern organizations.

Chapter 2 of 'Green from Green II - Businesses & Utilities' delves into the essential practice of auditing and analyzing energy use, a foundational step in the journey towards greener operations. By meticulously examining energy consumption, managers can uncover inefficiencies, identify key areas for improvement, and make informed decisions that propel their organizations towards sustainability.

Energy audits are not merely an exercise in data collection; they are a strategic endeavor that offers insights into the very pulse of an organization's energy use. Conducting comprehensive energy audits allows managers to gain a granular understanding of where energy is consumed, how it is used, and where waste occurs. This chapter will guide you through the process of conducting these audits, providing you with the tools and methodologies necessary to gather accurate and actionable data. From the initial scoping of the audit to the detailed analysis of energy flows, every step is crucial in building a robust energy management framework. Key to any effective energy audit is the identification of major energy consumption areas. Whether it is lighting, HVAC systems, manufacturing processes, or office equipment, pinpointing the primary energy consumers within your organization is vital.

This chapter will help you identify these critical areas, offering practical tips and techniques to ensure no stone is left unturned. By focusing on these key areas, you can prioritize actions and allocate resources where they will have the most significant impact.

In today's technologically advanced world, utilizing Energy Management Systems (EMS) has become indispensable. These sophisticated systems offer real-time data monitoring, advanced analytics, and automated controls that can significantly enhance the efficiency of energy management. This chapter will introduce you to the various types of EMS available, their features, and how to implement them effectively within your organization. Leveraging these systems not only streamlines the auditing process but also provides ongoing insights that can help sustain energy savings over the long term.

Analyzing energy data is another critical component of the auditing process. Data analysis transforms raw data into meaningful insights, enabling managers to make informed decisions about energy use and conservation measures. This chapter will equip you with some insights into the analytical tools and techniques needed to interpret energy data accurately. From basic statistical overview to more advanced methodologies, you will learn how to draw actionable conclusions that drive energy efficiency. To bring these concepts to life, we will explore case studies of successful energy audits.

These real-world examples highlight best practices, common challenges, and innovative solutions that have led to significant energy savings. By learning from these success stories, you can apply proven strategies to your own organization, avoiding common pitfalls and accelerating your path to sustainability.

As we embark on this journey through Chapter 2, keep in mind that energy auditing and analysis is not a one-time event but an ongoing process. Continuous monitoring, regular audits, and iterative improvements are essential to maintaining and enhancing energy efficiency. With the knowledge and strategies presented in this chapter, you will be well-equipped to lead your organization towards a more efficient, sustainable, and prosperous future. Welcome to the world of energy consumption auditing and analysis—where data-driven decisions unlock the potential for significant environmental and economic gains. Let's dive in and start transforming the way your organization uses energy, one audit at a time.

2.1 Conducting Comprehensive Energy Audits
In the quest for sustainability, the first and most crucial step is to conduct comprehensive energy audits.

Now I know that the term audit has some terrifying connotations, especially when it comes to taxes and such! An energy audit, however, is simply a systematic inspection and analysis of energy use, which helps identify opportunities for energy conservation and efficiency improvements. It provides a clear picture of where, how, and why energy is being consumed and highlights areas for potential savings. This process is pivotal for organizations keen on reducing their carbon footprint and optimizing operational costs, setting the foundation for all subsequent green initiatives.

Understanding the Scope and Objectives of an Energy Audit
Before diving into the methodologies of conducting an energy audit, it's essential to understand its scope and objectives. The primary goal of an energy audit is to identify where energy is being wasted and to recommend measures to enhance energy efficiency. However, the scope can vary significantly depending on the organization's size, industry, and specific needs. For instance, a manufacturing plant may focus on machinery and production processes, while an office building might concentrate more on HVAC systems and lighting.

The objectives can be broken down into several key areas:

1. Establishing a baseline of current energy consumption.
2. Identifying energy-saving opportunities.
3. Prioritizing energy efficiency measures based on cost-effectiveness.
4. Developing a detailed action plan for implementation.
5. Monitoring progress and adjusting strategies as needed.

Types of Energy Audits

Energy audits can be categorized into three main types: Preliminary (Walk-Through) Audits, General Audits, and Detailed (Investment-Grade) Audits.

1. <u>Preliminary (Walk-Through) Audits</u>: This is the most basic level of audit, involving a simple walk-through of the facility to identify obvious areas of energy waste. It provides a quick snapshot of potential improvements but lacks the depth and precision of more comprehensive audits.
2. <u>General Audits:</u> A more in-depth analysis, a general audit includes a detailed examination of energy consumption patterns, utility bills, and major energy-consuming equipment. This type of audit typically involves some level of data logging and analysis to identify key areas for improvement.
3. <u>Detailed (Investment-Grade) Audits:</u> The most comprehensive type of audit, detailed audits involve extensive data collection and analysis, often requiring several weeks or months to complete. They provide a thorough understanding of energy use, detailed recommendations for energy-saving measures, and a financial analysis of potential investments.

Preparing for an Energy Audit

Preparation is key to conducting an effective energy audit. The following steps should be taken to ensure a smooth and comprehensive audit process:

1. Assemble an Audit Team: An effective audit team should include members with diverse expertise, such as facilities managers, energy managers, engineers, and financial analysts. External consultants with specialized knowledge may also be brought in to provide additional insights.
2. Gather Historical Energy Data: Collecting utility bills, energy consumption records, and other relevant data for at least the past year is crucial. This historical data helps establish a baseline and identify trends or anomalies in energy use.
3. Identify Key Areas of Focus: Based on preliminary observations and historical data, pinpoint the areas or systems that are likely to offer the most significant energy-saving opportunities. This prioritization helps streamline the audit process and ensures that resources are focused on the most impactful areas.
4. Develop a Data Collection Plan: Outline the specific data that needs to be collected during the audit, such as equipment operating hours, energy consumption of individual systems, and environmental conditions.

Determine the methods and tools required for data collection, such as data loggers, meters, and sensors.

Conducting the On-Site Audit

The on-site audit is the heart of the energy audit process, where data collection and analysis take place. This stage involves several key activities:

1. Visual Inspection: Conduct a thorough walk-through of the facility to observe energy-consuming equipment, operational practices, and building conditions. Pay attention to obvious signs of energy waste, such as outdated lighting fixtures, poorly insulated areas, and malfunctioning equipment.
2. Data Logging and Monitoring: Use data loggers, meters, and sensors to measure the energy consumption of individual systems and equipment. This data provides valuable insights into how energy is used and where inefficiencies may exist. Monitor energy use over a representative period, typically ranging from a few weeks to several months if data is available, to capture variations in usage patterns.
3. Interview Staff and Operators: Engage with facility staff and equipment operators to gain a deeper understanding of operational practices, equipment performance, and potential areas for improvement. These conversations can reveal valuable insights that may not be immediately apparent from data alone.
4. Analyze Energy Consumption: Analyze the collected data to identify patterns, trends, and anomalies in energy use. Compare actual energy consumption with expected values based on equipment specifications and operational schedules. This analysis helps pinpoint specific areas where energy is being wasted.

Identifying Energy-Saving / Improvement Opportunities

Once the data has been collected and analyzed, the next step is to identify specific energy-saving or improvement opportunities. These opportunities can be categorized into three main types: operational improvements, maintenance measures, and capital investments.

1. Operational Improvements: These are changes to operational practices that can be implemented with minimal or no cost. Examples include adjusting thermostat settings, optimizing equipment schedules to avoid

peak rate energy usage, and implementing energy-saving behaviors among staff.
2. <u>Maintenance Measures:</u> Regular maintenance of equipment can significantly improve energy efficiency. This includes cleaning and servicing HVAC systems, repairing leaks in compressed air systems, and replacing worn-out components.
3. <u>Capital Investments:</u> These are larger-scale projects that require upfront investment but offer substantial long-term energy savings. Examples include upgrading to energy-efficient lighting, installing variable frequency drives (VFDs) on motors, and investing in renewable energy systems such as solar panels.

Developing an Action Plan

After identifying energy-saving opportunities, the next step is to develop a detailed action plan for implementation. This plan should include the following components:

1. <u>Prioritization:</u> Rank the identified opportunities based on factors such as potential energy savings, cost-effectiveness, and ease of implementation. Focus on the most impactful measures first to maximize benefits.
2. <u>Detailed Recommendations:</u> Provide detailed recommendations for each opportunity, including specific actions to be taken, estimated costs, and expected energy savings. Include technical specifications, vendor information, and any necessary approvals or permits.
3. <u>Implementation Timeline:</u> Outline a realistic timeline for implementing the recommended measures. Consider factors such as budget cycles, staffing availability, and potential disruptions to operations.
4. <u>Monitoring and Verification:</u> Establish a plan for monitoring and verifying the results of implemented measures. This includes tracking energy consumption, comparing actual savings with projected savings, and making adjustments as needed.

Reporting and Communication

Effective reporting and communication are essential to ensure that the findings and recommendations of the energy audit are understood and acted upon by all relevant stakeholders. The audit report should include the following elements:

1. <u>Executive Summary:</u> Summarize the key findings, recommendations, and expected benefits of the audit in a concise and accessible format.

Highlight the most significant energy-saving opportunities and their potential impact.
2. Detailed Findings: Provide a comprehensive overview of the audit process, including data collection methods, analysis results, and identified opportunities. Include technical details and supporting data to substantiate the findings.
3. Action Plan: Present the detailed action plan, including prioritized recommendations, implementation timeline, and monitoring plan. Clearly outline the next steps and responsibilities for moving forward.
4. Communication Strategy: Develop a communication strategy to share the audit findings and action plan with all relevant stakeholders, including senior management, facility staff, and external partners. Use a combination of written reports, presentations, and meetings to ensure that the information is effectively conveyed and understood.

Case Studies and Best Practices

To provide real-world examples and inspiration, including case studies and best practices from organizations that have successfully conducted energy audits and implemented energy-saving measures. These case studies should highlight the following:

1. Background: Provide an overview of the organization, its energy consumption profile, and the motivations for conducting the energy audit.
2. Audit Process: Describe the steps taken during the audit process, including data collection, analysis, and identification of opportunities.
3. Implemented Measures: Detail the specific energy-saving measures that were implemented, including any challenges faced and how they were overcome.
4. Results: Present the results of the implemented measures, including actual energy savings, cost savings, and other benefits such as improved operational efficiency and reduced environmental impact.
5. Lessons Learned: Share any lessons learned and best practices that can be applied to other organizations. Highlight key takeaways and recommendations for conducting successful energy audits.

Leveraging Technology and Innovation

In today's rapidly evolving technological landscape, leveraging technology and innovation can significantly enhance the effectiveness of energy audits. Consider the following advancements:

1. Advanced Metering Infrastructure (AMI): AMI systems provide real-time data on energy consumption, allowing for more accurate and detailed analysis. These systems can identify patterns and anomalies in energy use, enabling more targeted energy-saving measures.
2. Energy Management Systems (EMS): EMS platforms integrate data from various sources, providing a centralized dashboard for monitoring and managing energy consumption. These systems can automate data collection, analysis, and reporting, streamlining the audit process.
3. Internet of Things (IoT): IoT devices, such as smart sensors and connected equipment, can provide continuous monitoring of energy use and equipment performance. This data can be used to identify inefficiencies and optimize operations in real-time.
4. Data Analytics and Machine Learning: Advanced data analytics and machine learning algorithms can analyze large volumes of energy data to identify patterns, predict energy consumption, and recommend energy-saving measures. These technologies can provide insights that may not be immediately apparent through traditional analysis methods.

Building a Culture of Energy Efficiency

Finally, conducting a comprehensive energy audit is just the beginning. To sustain long-term energy savings, it's essential to build a culture of energy efficiency within the organization. Consider the following strategies:

1. Leadership Commitment: Ensure that senior management is committed to energy efficiency and sustainability. Their support is crucial for securing resources, driving initiatives, and motivating staff.
2. Employee Engagement: Engage employees at all levels in energy-saving initiatives. Provide training, resources, and incentives to encourage energy-efficient behaviors and practices.
3. Continuous Improvement: Not much different from any of the International Standards, this approach establishes a continuous improvement process for energy management. Regularly review energy performance, review the status of improvement opportunities, set new goals, and update the action plan based on ongoing monitoring and feedback.
4. Recognition and Rewards: Recognize and reward individuals and teams that contribute to energy-saving efforts. This can help reinforce the importance of energy efficiency and motivate others to get involved.

By conducting comprehensive energy audits and implementing the identified opportunities, organizations can achieve significant energy savings, reduce their environmental impact, and enhance their overall sustainability.

Pinpointing Energy Hotspots: A Comprehensive Guide

In the quest for sustainable energy management, identifying key areas of energy consumption is paramount. This process, often referred to as pinpointing energy hotspots, involves a meticulous examination of various aspects of your organization's energy use. By strategically focusing on these hotspots, managers can drive significant improvements in energy efficiency and cost savings, while simultaneously reducing the organization's carbon footprint.

This section investigates the techniques and methodologies for identifying these critical areas and provides actionable insights to aid in the effective management of energy consumption.

Understanding Energy Hotspots

An energy hotspot is a specific area within an organization where energy consumption is notably high. These hotspots can exist in various forms, such as specific departments, processes, or even individual pieces of equipment. The identification of these hotspots is essential for developing targeted strategies that can lead to substantial energy savings. Understanding the nature and characteristics of energy hotspots involves analyzing energy usage patterns, peak demand periods, and the operational context in which energy is consumed.

Conducting the Energy Audit

The first step in identifying energy hotspots is to conduct a comprehensive energy audit. An energy audit is a systematic approach to evaluate how energy is used within an organization. This is a process that involves collecting data on energy consumption, analyzing this data to identify patterns and trends, and pinpointing areas where energy use is disproportionately high or there are specific improvement opportunities, possibly using new technologies.

To remind, there are three levels of energy audits: a preliminary audit, a general audit, and an investment-grade audit. Each level provides a different depth of analysis, from a broad overview to a detailed examination that includes financial analysis and investment recommendations.

Utilizing Advanced Metering Infrastructure (AMI)

Advanced Metering Infrastructure (AMI) plays a crucial role in identifying energy hotspots. AMI systems provide real-time data on energy use, allowing managers to monitor consumption patterns with precision.

By leveraging AMI, organizations can gain insights into peak demand periods, energy wastage, and operational inefficiencies. The data gathered through AMI can be used to create detailed energy profiles for different areas of the organization, facilitating the identification of hotspots and enabling targeted interventions.

Analyzing Energy Consumption Data

Once data has been collected through an energy audit and AMI, the next step is to analyze this data to identify energy hotspots. This involves examining energy use across different time periods, departments, and processes. Statistical tools and software can be used to visualize energy consumption patterns, making it easier to spot anomalies and high-consumption areas.

Key metrics to consider include energy intensity (energy use per unit of output), load profiles, and peak demand periods. By analyzing these metrics, managers can identify areas where energy use is excessive and prioritize them for intervention.

Identifying High-Consumption Equipment and Processes

Certain pieces of equipment and processes are often responsible for a significant portion of an organization's energy consumption. Identifying these high-consumption elements is critical for effective energy management. Common culprits include HVAC systems, industrial machinery, lighting, and IT infrastructure. Detailed monitoring and analysis of these elements can reveal inefficiencies and opportunities for improvement.

For instance, outdated equipment may consume more energy than newer, more efficient models, and certain processes may be optimized to reduce energy use. Also, certain areas may be suspect, leakage on air systems, for example, or, the timing of charging systems during peak energy prices may also be another culprit.

Engaging Stakeholders in the Process

Successful identification of energy hotspots requires the involvement of various stakeholders within the organization. Engaging employees, managers, other key personnel and maybe even supply chain, or customers. in the process ensures that diverse perspectives are considered and that there is buy-in for energy-saving initiatives. Workshops, surveys, and collaborative meetings can be used to gather input and identify areas of concern. By fostering a culture of energy awareness and collaboration, organizations can more effectively pinpoint hotspots and implement sustainable practices.

Leveraging Technology for Detailed Analysis
Technology can significantly enhance the process of identifying energy hotspots. Energy management software, IoT devices, and machine learning algorithms can provide detailed insights into energy use and highlight areas of inefficiency.

For example, IoT sensors can monitor equipment performance in real time, while machine learning algorithms can predict future energy consumption patterns and identify potential hotspots before they become critical issues. By leveraging these technologies, organizations can achieve a more granular understanding of their energy use and develop more effective strategies for reducing consumption.

Case Studies and Real-World Examples
To illustrate the process of identifying energy hotspots, this section includes case studies and real-world examples of organizations that have successfully pinpointed and addressed high-consumption areas. These examples provide valuable lessons and insights that can be applied to other organizations. For instance, a manufacturing company may discover that its HVAC system is responsible for a significant portion of energy use and implement measures such as upgrading to more efficient units or optimizing operational schedules. Similarly, an office building might identify lighting as a major energy consumer and adopt strategies such as installing LED lights and implementing smart lighting controls.

Developing a Plan of Action
Once energy hotspots have been identified, the next step is to develop a plan of action to address them. This plan should include specific, measurable objectives, timelines, and responsibilities.

Key elements of the plan may include upgrading equipment, optimizing processes, implementing energy-saving technologies, and engaging employees in energy conservation efforts. It is also important to establish a system for monitoring progress and evaluating the effectiveness of interventions. By developing a comprehensive plan of action, organizations can systematically address energy hotspots and achieve long-term energy savings.

Continuous Improvement and Monitoring
Identifying energy hotspots is not a one-time activity but an ongoing process.

Continuous monitoring and improvement are essential to ensure that energy-saving measures remain effective and that new hotspots are promptly identified and addressed. Regular energy audits, real-time monitoring, and periodic reviews of energy consumption data are critical components of this process. Additionally, organizations should stay informed about new technologies and best practices in energy management to continually enhance their strategies.

Pinpointing energy hotspots is a foundational step in the journey towards sustainable energy management. By thoroughly understanding and addressing key areas of energy consumption, organizations can achieve significant reductions in energy use, cost savings, and environmental impact.

This section has provided a comprehensive guide to identifying energy hotspots, from conducting energy audits and utilizing advanced metering infrastructure to engaging stakeholders and leveraging technology. By following these best practices, managers can lead their organizations towards a greener, more sustainable future.

2.2 Harnessing the Power of Energy Management Systems (EMS) for Optimal Efficiency

In the journey towards sustainable management, harnessing the power of Energy Management Systems (EMS) stands as a pivotal strategy. EMS is an integrated approach that leverages technology and best practices to monitor, control, and optimize energy usage across an organization. By implementing EMS, managers can achieve significant reductions in energy consumption, operational costs, and environmental impact.

This section delves into the multifaceted aspects of EMS, offering a comprehensive guide on its benefits, implementation, and optimization. Understanding Energy Management Systems (EMS)

At its core, an Energy Management System (EMS) is a combination of hardware, software, and processes designed to collect, analyze, and manage energy data. EMS provides real-time insights into energy usage patterns, enabling managers to make informed decisions about energy consumption and efficiency.

By integrating EMS into their operations, organizations can identify energy-saving opportunities, track performance, and ensure compliance with sustainability goals.

Components of an Effective EMS

An effective EMS comprises several key components that work together to deliver optimal results:

<u>Energy Monitoring Devices:</u> These devices, such as smart meters and sensors, collect data on energy usage in real-time. They provide granular insights into energy consumption at various levels, from individual equipment to entire facilities.

<u>Data Management Software:</u> This software aggregates and analyzes the data collected by monitoring devices. It generates reports, visualizations, and alerts, helping managers to identify trends, anomalies, and areas for improvement.

<u>Control Systems:</u> These systems enable automated control of energy-consuming devices. For example, they can adjust lighting, HVAC systems, and machinery based on predefined criteria, such as occupancy, time of day, or ambient conditions.

User Interface: A user-friendly interface allows managers to interact with the EMS, set parameters, and access reports. It should be intuitive, customizable, and accessible from various devices, including computers, tablets, and smartphones.

Benefits of Implementing EMS

The implementation of an EMS offers numerous benefits that can transform an organization's energy management practices:

Enhanced Energy Efficiency: By providing real-time insights and control over energy usage, EMS helps identify inefficiencies and implement corrective measures. This leads to significant reductions in energy consumption and costs.

Improved Operational Performance: EMS enables proactive maintenance and optimization of equipment, reducing downtime and extending the lifespan of assets.

Regulatory Compliance: EMS helps organizations comply with energy regulations and standards, such as ISO 50001, by providing accurate data and documentation.

Environmental Impact: By reducing energy consumption and emissions, EMS contributes to an organization's sustainability goals and minimizes its carbon footprint.

Cost Savings: The combination of reduced energy consumption, improved operational performance, and compliance with regulations all translate into substantial cost savings over time – however, the up-front assumptions and calculations for a Return On Investment (ROI) justification must be carefully prepared and presented to approval.

Implementing an EMS - Step-by-Step Guide

Implementing an EMS requires careful planning and execution. The following is some outline guidance to help managers navigate the process:

1. Conduct a Preliminary Energy Audit Before implementing an EMS, it is essential to conduct a preliminary energy audit to assess the current energy consumption and identify areas for improvement. This audit provides a baseline for measuring the impact of the EMS and helps prioritize energy-saving opportunities.

2. <u>Define Objectives and Metrics</u> Clearly define the objectives and metrics for the EMS implementation. Objectives may include reducing energy consumption, improving operational efficiency, and achieving regulatory compliance. Metrics should be specific, measurable, achievable, relevant, and time-bound (SMART).

3. <u>Select the Right EMS Solution</u> Choose an EMS solution that aligns with your organization's needs and objectives. Consider factors such as scalability, compatibility with existing systems, ease of use, and vendor support. Evaluate different options through demonstrations, trials, and references from other organizations.

4. <u>Install Energy Monitoring Devices</u> Install energy monitoring devices, such as smart meters and sensors, at key points throughout the facility. Ensure that these devices are calibrated and integrated with the data management software to provide accurate and reliable data.

5. <u>Configure the Data Management Software</u> Configure the data management software to collect, analyze, and report energy data. Set up custom dashboards, alerts, and reports that provide actionable insights and are relevant to your operations. Ensure that the software is accessible to authorized personnel and integrated with other systems as needed.

6. <u>Train Staff and Stakeholders</u> Provide training to staff and stakeholders on how to use the EMS effectively. This includes understanding the data, interpreting reports, and making informed decisions based on the insights provided by the system. Encourage a culture of energy awareness and continuous improvement.

7. <u>Monitor and Optimize</u> Continuously monitor the EMS to ensure it is functioning correctly and delivering the desired results. Use the data and insights to identify areas for improvement and implement corrective measures. Regularly review and update the system to adapt to changing needs and technologies.

Case Study: Successful EMS Implementation
To illustrate the benefits of EMS, consider the case of a manufacturing company that implemented an EMS across its facilities. The company conducted a preliminary energy audit and identified several areas of inefficiency, including outdated lighting systems, poorly maintained HVAC

equipment, and lack of energy awareness among staff. By implementing an EMS, the company was able to:

Reduce Energy Consumption: The EMS provided real-time insights into energy usage, allowing the company to identify and address inefficiencies. As a result, energy consumption was reduced by 20% within the first year.

Improve Equipment Performance: The EMS enabled proactive maintenance and optimization of equipment, reducing downtime and extending the lifespan of assets. This led to improved operational performance and cost savings.

Achieve Regulatory Compliance: The EMS helped the company comply with energy regulations and standards, such as ISO 50001, by providing accurate data and documentation. This ensured that the company met its sustainability goals and minimized its environmental impact and increased credibility for marketing.

Encourage Energy Awareness: The EMS provided valuable insights and reports that were shared with staff and stakeholders. This encouraged a culture of energy awareness and continuous improvement, further enhancing the company's energy management practices.

Challenges and Considerations

While the benefits of EMS are significant, there are also challenges and considerations to keep in mind:

Initial Investment: Implementing an EMS requires an upfront investment in hardware, software, and training. However, the long-term cost savings and benefits often outweigh the initial costs.

Integration with Existing Systems: Ensuring compatibility and integration with existing systems can be complex. It is essential to choose an EMS solution that is flexible and can work seamlessly with other systems and processes.

Data Security: Protecting the data collected by the EMS is crucial. Implement robust security measures to safeguard sensitive information and ensure compliance with data protection regulations.

Change Management: Implementing an EMS involves changes in processes, behaviors, and culture. Effective change management strategies, including communication, training, and stakeholder engagement, are essential for successful implementation.

Future Trends in EMS

The field of energy management is continually evolving, with new technologies and trends shaping the future of EMS:

Artificial Intelligence (AI) and Machine Learning: AI and machine learning algorithms can analyze vast amounts of energy data to identify patterns, predict future consumption, and optimize energy usage. These technologies can enhance the capabilities of EMS and provide more accurate and actionable insights.

Internet of Things (IoT) Integration: The integration of IoT devices with EMS allows for more granular monitoring and control of energy usage. IoT devices can provide real-time data from various sources, enabling more precise and efficient energy management.

Cloud-Based Solutions: Cloud-based EMS solutions offer scalability, flexibility, and accessibility. They allow organizations to access and manage energy data from anywhere, facilitating remote monitoring and control.

Blockchain Technology: Blockchain can enhance the transparency, security, and traceability of energy transactions. It can be used to verify energy consumption, track renewable energy certificates, and facilitate peer-to-peer energy trading.

Decentralized Energy Systems: The rise of decentralized energy systems, such as microgrids and renewable energy sources, presents new opportunities for EMS. These systems can be integrated with EMS to optimize energy generation, storage, and consumption.

To conclude this section, harnessing the power of Energy Management Systems (EMS) is a critical strategy for managers seeking to enhance energy efficiency, reduce costs, and achieve sustainability goals. By understanding the components, benefits, and implementation process of EMS, managers can effectively leverage this technology to drive significant improvements in their organization's energy management practices. As the field continues to evolve, staying informed about emerging trends and technologies will ensure that organizations remain at the forefront of sustainable energy management.

Green from Green II - Businesses & Utilities

2.3 Analyzing Energy Data for Informed Decision-Making

In the quest to achieve sustainable management, the effective analysis of energy data stands as a cornerstone.

Energy data analysis is not merely about crunching numbers; it is about transforming raw data into actionable insights that drive strategic decisions. This process involves a meticulous examination of energy consumption patterns, identification of inefficiencies, and the development of targeted strategies to optimize usage. By leveraging advanced analytical tools and methodologies, managers can make informed decisions that align with sustainability goals while also enhancing operational efficiency.

Understanding Energy Data: The Foundation

The first step in energy data analysis is to understand the types of data available and their significance. Energy data can be categorized into several types, including consumption data, cost data, and performance data. Consumption data tracks the amount of energy used over a specific period, cost data relates to the financial expenditure on energy, and performance data measures the efficiency of energy use to output.

Types of Energy Data

- Consumption Data: This includes information on the total energy used, peak demand periods, and usage patterns over time. It helps in identifying high-consumption areas and understanding the temporal dynamics of energy use.
- Cost Data: Analyzing the financial aspects of energy consumption, such as monthly bills, tariff structures, and cost variations, provides insights into the economic impact of energy use.
- Performance Data: This data assesses the efficiency of energy use by comparing the energy input to the output. It includes metrics such as Energy Use Intensity (EUI) and Specific Energy Consumption (SEC).

Sources of Energy Data

- Utility Bills: Monthly utility bills provide a wealth of information on energy consumption and cost. They are a primary source for historical data analysis.
- Energy Management Systems (EMS): These systems provide real-time data on energy use, enabling continuous monitoring and analysis.
- Submetering: Installing submeters allows for detailed tracking of energy

use in specific areas or process equipment, providing granular data for analysis.

Data Collection - The Starting Point
Effective energy data analysis begins with accurate and comprehensive data collection. This involves gathering data from various sources, ensuring its accuracy, and organizing it in a manner that facilitates analysis.

Steps in Data Collection:
1. Identify Data Sources: Determine the sources of energy data, such as utility bills, EMS, and submeters.
2. Establish Data Collection Procedures: Define the processes for collecting data, including frequency (daily, weekly, monthly), methods (manual, automated), and tools (spreadsheets, software).
3. Ensure Data Accuracy: Implement measures to verify the accuracy of the collected data, such as cross-referencing with utility bills and calibrating meters.
4. Organize Data: Structure the data in a format that facilitates analysis, such as categorizing it by time, location, or equipment.

Data Analysis Techniques - Turning Data into Insights
Once the data is collected, the next step is to analyze it using various techniques to uncover patterns, trends, and anomalies. This analysis provides the insights needed to make informed decisions.

Descriptive Analytics
Descriptive analytics involves summarizing historical energy data to understand past consumption patterns. Techniques include:

- Trend Analysis: Examining energy consumption over time to identify trends and seasonal variations.
- Benchmarking: Comparing energy use against industry standards or similar organizations to assess performance.
- Load Profiling: Analyzing the load profile to understand how energy use varies throughout the day or week.

Diagnostic Analytics
Diagnostic analytics seeks to understand the reasons behind specific energy consumption patterns. Techniques include:

- Root Cause Analysis: Identifying the underlying causes of high energy use

or inefficiencies.
- Correlation Analysis: Examining the relationships between different variables, such as the impact of weather conditions on energy use.

Predictive Analytics
Predictive analytics uses historical data to forecast future energy consumption. Techniques include:

- Regression Analysis: Developing models to predict energy use based on various factors, such as production levels or weather conditions.
- Time Series Analysis: Forecasting future energy consumption based on historical trends.

Prescriptive Analytics
Prescriptive analytics provides recommendations for optimizing energy use. Techniques include:

- Optimization Models: Developing models to identify the optimal energy use strategies, such as load shifting or demand response.
- Scenario Analysis: Evaluating the impact of different strategies on energy consumption and costs.

Leveraging Technology for Data Analysis

Advanced technologies play a crucial role in enhancing the accuracy and efficiency of energy data analysis. From software tools to Internet of Things (IoT) devices, technology provides the capabilities needed to transform data into actionable insights.

Energy Management Software:
Energy management software integrates various data sources and provides tools for analysis, visualization, and reporting. Key features can include:

- Data Integration: Combining data from multiple sources, such as utility bills, EMS, and submeters.
- Real-Time Monitoring: Providing real-time data on energy use, enabling continuous monitoring and immediate response to anomalies.
- Visualization Tools: Offering graphical representations of data, such as charts and dashboards, to facilitate analysis.
- Reporting Capabilities: Generating reports that summarize key findings and provide actionable recommendations.

IoT and Smart Devices
IoT devices, such as smart meters and sensors, provide real-time data on energy use and environmental conditions. Benefits include:

- Real-Time Data Collection: Enabling continuous monitoring of energy use and immediate detection of anomalies.
- Granular Data: Providing detailed data on specific areas or equipment, facilitating targeted analysis.
- Remote Monitoring: Allowing managers to monitor energy use from anywhere, enhancing flexibility and responsiveness.

Case Study: Data-Driven Decision-Making in Action
To illustrate the power of energy data analysis, consider the case of a manufacturing facility that implemented a comprehensive energy management program.

By leveraging advanced data collection and analysis techniques, the facility achieved significant improvements in energy efficiency.

1. Data Collection The facility began by installing submeters to track energy use in different departments and for specific equipment. They also integrated data from utility bills and the EMS into a centralized energy management software.
2. Descriptive Analytics The data was analyzed to identify consumption patterns and benchmark performance against industry standards. This revealed that the facility's energy use was higher than average, particularly during peak demand periods.
3. Diagnostic Analytics A root cause analysis identified several factors contributing to high energy use, including inefficient equipment, suboptimal operational practices, and poor insulation in certain areas.
4. Predictive Analytics Regression models were developed to forecast future energy use based on production levels and weather conditions. This enabled the facility to anticipate peak demand periods and plan accordingly.
5. Prescriptive Analytics Optimization models and scenario analysis were used to develop strategies for reducing energy use, such as upgrading equipment, improving insulation, and implementing demand response programs.

Results
By implementing these strategies, the facility achieved a 20% reduction in energy consumption and a significant decrease in energy costs. The real-time monitoring capabilities also enabled immediate detection and response to anomalies, further enhancing efficiency.

Conclusion: The Path to Informed Decision-Making

The analysis of energy data is a critical component of sustainable management. By understanding the types of data available, implementing effective data collection procedures, and leveraging advanced analytical techniques and technologies, managers can transform raw data into actionable insights. These insights enable informed decision-making that not only aligns with sustainability goals but also enhances operational efficiency and reduces costs.

In the 2020s and beyond, the ability to analyze energy data effectively will be a key differentiator for organizations striving to achieve sustainable success.

2.4 Case Studies - Successful Energy Audits

Introduction to Case Studies

In this section, we will dive into real-world examples of successful energy audits. By examining these case studies, we can glean valuable insights into the methodologies applied, the challenges encountered, and the impactful outcomes achieved.

These typical examples should serve as a testament to the transformative potential of energy audits when conducted with precision and foresight noting that the studies are from various sources and the names have been changed to protect the innocent - JH.

Case Study 1: The Manufacturing Marvel

Background
Our first case study focuses on a mid-sized manufacturing company located in the Midwest. This company, producing automotive components, faced escalating energy costs and sought to improve its operational efficiency. The management team decided to undertake a comprehensive energy audit to identify areas for improvement.

Audit Methodology
The audit was conducted in three phases:

1. Pre-Audit Preparation: The team collected data on energy consumption

patterns, historical utility bills, and operational schedules. This preliminary analysis helped in understanding the baseline energy usage.
2. On-Site Inspection: A team of certified energy managers from the AEE inspected the facility. They used advanced diagnostic tools, such as thermal imaging cameras and ultrasonic leak detectors, to identify inefficiencies.
3. Data Analysis and Reporting: The collected data was analyzed using specialized software to pinpoint areas of excessive energy use. The final report included a detailed breakdown of energy consumption, potential savings, and recommended actions.

Key Findings

The audit revealed several critical findings:

1. Inefficient Lighting: The facility used outdated fluorescent lighting, which consumed a significant amount of energy.
2. Compressed Air Leaks: Numerous leaks in the compressed air system were identified, leading to substantial energy wastage.
3. Poor Insulation: Certain sections of the plant had inadequate insulation, causing higher heating and cooling costs.
4. Outdated Equipment: Several machines were operating below optimal efficiency levels due to age and lack of maintenance.

Implementation and Tangible Results

Based on the audit recommendations, the company took the following actions:

1. Lighting Upgrade: Replaced fluorescent lights with energy-efficient LED lighting, reducing lighting energy consumption by 50%.
2. Compressed Air System Maintenance: Sealed all identified leaks and installed an automated monitoring system to detect future leaks, resulting in a 20% reduction in energy use.
3. Insulation Improvement: Upgraded insulation in critical areas, leading to a 15% decrease in heating and cooling costs.
4. Equipment Modernization: Replaced outdated machines with energy-efficient models, enhancing overall productivity and reducing energy consumption by 10%.

The combined efforts were reported to have led to a 25% reduction in total energy costs, translating to annual savings of $200,000.

Case Study 2: A Retail Giant

Background

This case study examines a national retail chain with over 500 stores across one G7 country. The company aimed to reduce its carbon footprint and operational costs by conducting energy audits in its top 50 energy-consuming locations.

Audit Methodology

The audit was executed in the following steps:

1. Initial Assessment: The energy management team conducted a preliminary review of energy usage across all locations to identify the top energy-consuming stores.
2. Site Visits: Each of the 50 selected stores underwent a thorough on-site inspection. The audit team evaluated HVAC systems, lighting, refrigeration units, and building envelopes.
3. Energy Modeling: Advanced energy modelling software was used to simulate various energy-saving measures and predict their impact on consumption.

Key Findings

The audits uncovered several areas for improvement:

1. HVAC Inefficiencies: Many stores had older HVAC systems that were not operating efficiently.
2. Refrigeration Units: Refrigeration units in some stores were outdated and consumed excessive energy.
3. Lighting: Like the first case study, many stores used inefficient lighting systems.
4. Building Envelope: Poor insulation and air leaks were common issues across multiple locations.

Implementation and Tangible Results

The retail chain implemented a series of energy-saving measures based on the audit findings:

1. HVAC System Overhaul: Upgraded to high-efficiency HVAC systems, resulting in a 30% reduction in HVAC-related energy consumption.
2. Refrigeration Unit Replacement: Installed energy-efficient refrigeration units, cutting refrigeration energy use by 25%.
3. Lighting Retrofit: Transitioned to LED lighting in all audited stores,

achieving a 40% reduction in lighting energy consumption.
4. Building Envelope Improvements: Enhanced insulation and sealed air leaks, leading to a 15% reduction in overall energy costs.

The combined measures led to an average energy cost reduction of 20% per store, with total annual savings estimated at $5 million across all 50 locations.

Case Study 3: The Educational Institution

Background
Our final case study highlights a university campus in California. The university aimed to achieve carbon neutrality by 2030 and decided to start with a comprehensive energy audit of its facilities.

Audit Methodology
The audit was divided into four phases:

1. Data Collection: The team gathered extensive data on energy usage across various buildings, including dormitories, academic buildings, and recreational facilities.
2. On-Site Inspection: Certified energy managers conducted detailed inspections of HVAC systems, lighting, water heating systems, and renewable energy installations.
3. Stakeholder Engagement: The audit team engaged with faculty, staff, and students to understand their energy usage patterns and gather input on potential improvements.
4. Data Analysis and Reporting: The collected data was analyzed, and a comprehensive report was generated, highlighting key findings and recommendations.

Key Findings
The audit identified the following critical areas and improvement opportunities:

1. HVAC System Inefficiencies: Many buildings had HVAC systems that were not optimized for energy efficiency.
2. Lighting: Outdated lighting systems were prevalent across the campus.
3. Water Heating: Inefficient water heating systems were a significant energy drain.
4. Renewable Energy Potential: The campus had untapped potential for solar energy installations – particularly unused rooftops.

Implementation and Results
The university implemented a multi-faceted approach based on the audit findings:

1. HVAC System Optimization: Conducted a campus-wide HVAC system upgrade, leading to a 25% reduction in HVAC-related energy consumption.
2. Lighting Retrofit: Replaced all outdated lighting with LED systems, resulting in a 35% reduction in lighting energy use.
3. Water Heating Improvements: Installed high-efficiency water heaters and implemented a solar water heating system, reducing water heating energy consumption by 30%.
4. Solar Energy Installation: Installed solar panels on rooftops and open spaces, generating 20% of the campus's energy needs from renewable sources.

The combined efforts resulted in approximately a 30% reduction in energy costs and positioned the university as a leader in sustainability in the sector.

Conclusion
These case studies underscore the importance of thorough energy audits and the substantial benefits they can bring to various sectors. From manufacturing and retail to education, the insights gained from these audits can lead to significant energy savings, cost reductions, and a smaller carbon footprint. By adopting similar methodologies and learning from these successful examples, managers can drive their organizations towards a more sustainable and efficient future.

2.5 Real-Life Success Stories in Energy Auditing and Analysis

In this section, we dig a bit deeper into the transformative power of energy auditing and analysis with more 'real-life' or typical stories from the industry. These stories highlight how organizations and individuals have leveraged comprehensive energy audits, identified key areas of energy consumption, utilized energy management systems, and analyzed energy data to make informed decisions.

The following case studies and stories serve as both inspiration and practical guidance for those looking to enhance their energy efficiency. Again, these typical examples should serve as a testament to the transformative potential of energy audits noting that the studies are from various sources and the names have been changed to protect the innocent.

Turning the Tide: The Story of Oceanic Industries' Energy Revolution

Oceanic Industries, a leading manufacturer of marine equipment, faced mounting pressure to reduce its energy consumption and carbon footprint. Located on the west coast, the company's sprawling facilities were notorious energy guzzlers.

In 2018, the company decided to conduct a comprehensive energy audit as part of its commitment to sustainability. The audit revealed that the manufacturing processes were the primary culprits, accounting for nearly 70% of the total energy consumption. The energy management team identified several key areas for improvement, including outdated machinery, inefficient lighting, and poor insulation.

Utilizing an Energy Management System (EMS), the team began monitoring energy usage in real time. The EMS provided granular data, pinpointing specific machines and areas where energy was being wasted. For instance, the data showed that the CNC machines were left running idle for hours, consuming unnecessary energy.

Armed with this information, the team implemented a series of strategic changes.

- The company they invested in modern, energy-efficient machinery, which reduced energy consumption by 25%.
- They upgraded the lighting system to LED, resulting in a 15% reduction in energy use.
- Insulation improvements in the facility's walls and ceilings further cut down heating and cooling costs by 10%.
- To ensure long-term success, Oceanic Industries integrated the EMS into their daily operations to provide continuous feedback and enable the team to make real-time adjustments and maintain optimal energy efficiency.

The results were astounding - within two years, the company had reduced its overall energy consumption by 40% and cut greenhouse gas emissions by 30%. Oceanic Industries not only saved millions of dollars in energy costs but also positioned itself as a leader in sustainable manufacturing.

The story shows how a comprehensive energy audit, coupled with strategic implementation and continuous monitoring, can lead to significant energy savings and environmental benefits.

Lighting the Way: GreenTech Solutions' Journey to Energy Efficiency

GreenTech Solutions, a mid-sized tech firm based in Texas, was known for its innovative products but their management team felt that they lagged in energy efficiency.

In 2019, the company's CEO, decided it was time for a change. He initiated a comprehensive energy audit to uncover inefficiencies and identify opportunities for improvement.

The audit revealed that the company's HVAC system was the primary energy consumer, accounting for nearly 50% of the total usage. Additionally, the office lighting and server rooms were significant contributors to the high energy bills.

- They decided to tackle these issues head-on and started by upgrading the HVAC system with energy-efficiency monitoring, which included smart thermostats and automated controls. This change alone resulted in a 20% reduction in energy consumption.
- Next, they replaced traditional fluorescent lights with LED lighting throughout the office, further cutting energy use by 15%.
- Recognizing the importance of data-driven decision-making, GreenTech Solutions implemented an advanced Energy Management System (EMS). The EMS provided real-time data on energy usage, helping the team identify patterns and areas for further improvement. For instance, the data revealed that the server rooms were constantly overcooled, wasting energy. By adjusting the temperature settings and optimizing airflow, they achieved an additional 10% reduction in energy consumption.

To ensure the success of these initiatives, the company also embarked on an employee engagement campaign. They educated staff about the importance of energy efficiency and encouraged them to adopt energy-saving practices, such as turning off lights and equipment when not in use. This cultural shift, combined with the technological upgrades, led to a remarkable transformation.

Within a year, GreenTech Solutions had reduced its overall energy consumption by 35% and significantly cut operating costs. The company also received accolades for its commitment to sustainability, enhancing its reputation and attracting new clients who valued eco-friendly practices. GreenTech Solutions' journey demonstrates the power of a holistic approach to energy auditing and analysis.

By addressing key areas of consumption, leveraging advanced technology, and fostering a culture of sustainability, the company achieved substantial energy savings and positioned itself as a forward-thinking leader in the tech industry.

From Red to Green: The Transformation of Central City Hospital

Central City Hospital, a bustling medical facility in the heart of a major metropolitan area, was grappling with skyrocketing energy costs and increasing pressure to reduce its carbon footprint.

In 2020, the hospital's board of directors decided to conduct a comprehensive energy audit to identify inefficiencies and explore improvement opportunities. The audit, conducted by a team of certified energy managers, revealed several critical improvement opportunities.

The hospital's HVAC system, lighting, and medical equipment were identified as the primary energy consumers. Additionally, the audit highlighted issues with building insulation and energy management practices. To address these challenges, the hospital implemented a multi-faceted energy management strategy.

- First, they upgraded the HVAC system to a high-efficiency model, incorporating advanced controls and automation. This change resulted in a 25% reduction in energy consumption.
- Next, they replaced outdated lighting with LED fixtures, achieving an additional 15% energy savings.
- Recognizing the importance of data-driven decision-making, Central City Hospital installed an Energy Management System (EMS) to monitor energy usage in real-time. The EMS provided valuable insights, such as identifying periods of peak energy consumption and pinpointing areas of inefficiency. For instance, the data revealed that the hospital's radiology department was using significantly more energy than necessary. By optimizing the equipment settings and scheduling maintenance during off-peak hours, the hospital achieved a 10% reduction in energy use.

The hospital also focused on improving building insulation, which helped reduce heating and cooling costs by 10%.

To support these initiatives, the hospital launched an employee engagement program, educating staff about energy conservation and encouraging them to adopt sustainable practices.

Within two years, Central City Hospital had reduced its overall energy consumption by 40%, significantly lowering operating costs. The hospital also received recognition for its commitment to sustainability, earning several awards and enhancing its reputation in the community.

By addressing key areas of energy consumption, leveraging advanced technology, and fostering a culture of sustainability, this hospital achieved substantial energy savings and demonstrated its commitment to environmental stewardship.

Conclusion: Mastering Energy Audits for Sustainable Management

In conclusion, conducting comprehensive energy audits is the cornerstone of effective energy management. By thoroughly assessing your facility's energy usage, you can identify key areas of energy consumption that offer the greatest opportunities for improvement.

Utilizing advanced Energy Management Systems (EMS) enables precise monitoring and control, allowing for real-time adjustments that can lead to significant energy savings. Analyzing energy data meticulously provides the insights necessary for informed decision-making, ensuring that your strategies are both effective and sustainable.

Several case studies highlighted the tangible benefits of successful energy audits, showcasing how organizations have achieved substantial cost savings and enhanced operational efficiency.

Key takeaways for readers include the importance of starting with a detailed energy audit, leveraging technology through EMS, and continuously analyzing data to refine strategies. By implementing these practices, managers can not only reduce energy consumption but also contribute significantly to environmental sustainability.

Remember, the journey towards energy efficiency is ongoing and requires a proactive approach, but the rewards—in terms of cost savings, operational efficiency, and environmental impact—are well worth the effort.

3 REDUCING EMISSIONS: STRATEGIES AND IMPLEMENTATION

Source: Pexels - Photo by Marcin Jozwiak:

As we navigate through the 2020s, the imperative to reduce emissions has never been more pressing. Climate change is no longer a distant threat but a present-day reality that demands immediate and decisive action. For managers committed to sustainability, the challenge lies not only in recognizing the gravity of the situation but also in implementing effective strategies to mitigate their organization's carbon footprint, while at the same time, keeping their operations profitable – that will take creativity and resilience.

This chapter, 'Reducing Emissions: Strategies and Implementation,' serves as your guide to understanding and addressing the multifaceted issue of emissions. Emissions, in their various forms, contribute significantly to the degradation of our environment.

From carbon dioxide (CO_2) to methane (CH_4) and nitrous oxide (N_2O), each type of emission plays a role in exacerbating global warming and climate change. Understanding the different types of emissions, often summarised in the marine industry as NOX, SOX and CO2, is the first step in developing targeted strategies for reduction. This chapter will examine some of the specifics, providing you with the foundational knowledge needed to identify and categorize the emissions pertinent to your organization.

Setting emission reduction goals is a critical component of any sustainability strategy. These goals should be ambitious yet achievable, aligned with global benchmarks such as the Paris Agreement, and subsequent COPXX's, and tailored to the unique circumstances of your organization. We will explore the process of setting these goals, including the importance of stakeholder engagement, the role of data in goal-setting, and the need for a clear timeline and milestones.

Once goals are established, the next step is to implement green technologies and practices. This chapter will introduce you to a range of innovative solutions designed to reduce emissions. From renewable energy sources such as solar and wind power to energy-efficient systems and sustainable supply chain practices, we will cover a spectrum of options that can be tailored to your organization's needs. Real-world examples and case studies throughout will illustrate how these technologies have been successfully implemented by leading companies across various industries.

Monitoring and reporting emission levels is crucial for maintaining transparency and accountability. Effective monitoring allows you to track progress, identify areas for improvement, and ensure compliance with regulatory requirements. This chapter will guide you through the best practices for monitoring emissions, including the use of advanced software tools and the importance of regular audits. We will also discuss the significance of transparent reporting, both internally and externally, to build trust with stakeholders and demonstrate your organization's commitment to sustainability.

Government incentives and grants can play a pivotal role in supporting your emission reduction efforts and indeed funding the projects that address your improvement opportunities. These financial aids can offset the initial costs of implementing green technologies and practices, making it more feasible for organizations to adopt sustainable solutions. This chapter will provide an overview of the various incentives and grants available, along with guidance on how to apply for them and maximize their benefits.

In conclusion, reducing emissions is a multifaceted challenge that requires a strategic, informed, and proactive approach. By understanding the different types of emissions, setting clear goals, implementing green technologies, monitoring progress, and leveraging government incentives, you can significantly reduce your organization's carbon footprint. This chapter will equip you with the knowledge and many of the tools needed to lead the way in emission reduction, paving the path towards a greener, more sustainable future.

3.1 Understanding Different Types of Emissions

Understanding the various types of emissions is crucial for any organization aiming to implement effective strategies for reduction. Emissions can be categorized into several types, each with distinct sources and impacts on the environment. By comprehensively understanding these emissions, managers can tailor their strategies to address specific challenges and opportunities unique to their operations.

Scope 1 Emissions - Direct Emissions

Scope 1 emissions are direct emissions from sources that are owned or controlled by the organization. These include emissions from combustion in owned or controlled boilers, furnaces, and vehicles, and emissions from chemical production in owned or controlled process equipment.

Stationary Combustion Sources

Stationary combustion sources include equipment and facilities such as boilers, furnaces, and engines that burn fuel to produce energy or heat. These are typically found in manufacturing plants, power generation facilities, and other industrial operations. The emissions from these sources primarily consist of carbon dioxide (CO_2), methane (CH_4), and nitrous oxide (N_2O).

Mobile Combustion Sources

Mobile combustion sources refer to vehicles and machinery that consume fuel for transportation and operational purposes. This includes company-owned cars, trucks, buses, and off-road equipment like forklifts and construction machinery. The primary emissions from these sources are CO_2, CH_4, and N_2O, along with other pollutants like sulphur dioxide (SO_2) and particulate matter (PM).

Fugitive Emissions

Fugitive emissions are unintended emissions that escape from equipment or processes, such as leaks from valves, joints, and connections in pipelines and storage tanks. These emissions are often overlooked but can be significant in industries like oil and gas, where methane leaks are a major concern.

Scope 2 Emissions - Indirect Emissions from Purchased Energy

Scope 2 emissions are indirect emissions from the generation of purchased electricity, steam, heating, and cooling consumed by the organization. Although these emissions occur at the facility where the energy is generated, they are attributed to the organization that consumes the energy.

Purchased Electricity
Electricity is a major source of emissions for many organizations. The carbon footprint of purchased electricity depends on the energy mix of the grid from which the electricity is sourced. For example, electricity generated from coal-fired power plants has a higher emission factor compared to electricity from renewable sources like wind or solar.

Purchased Steam, Heating, and Cooling
Organizations that purchase steam, heating, or cooling from external providers also contribute to Scope 2 emissions. These services are often generated using fossil fuels, resulting in CO_2, CH_4, and N_2O emissions. The extent of these emissions depends on the efficiency and energy mix of the service provider.

Scope 3 Emissions: Other Indirect Emissions

Scope 3 emissions encompass all other indirect emissions that occur in the value chain of the reporting company, including both upstream and downstream emissions. These are often the largest share of an organization's carbon footprint and can be challenging to measure and manage.

Upstream Emissions
Upstream emissions are those associated with the production and transportation of goods and services purchased by the organization. This includes emissions from the extraction of raw materials, manufacturing of products, and transportation to the organization's facilities. Examples include emissions from suppliers, business travel, and employee commuting.

Downstream Emissions
Downstream emissions occur after the product or service has left the organization's control. These can include emissions from the use of sold products, disposal of waste, and transportation and distribution of products to end-users. For instance, a company that manufactures appliances would

account for the emissions generated during the use of those appliances by consumers.

Greenhouse Gases (GHGs) and Their Impact

Understanding the specific greenhouse gases (GHGs) involved in emissions is essential for targeted reduction strategies. The primary GHGs include carbon dioxide (CO_2), methane (CH_4), nitrous oxide (N_2O), and fluorinated gases.

Carbon Dioxide (CO_2)
CO_2 is the most prevalent GHG, primarily released through the burning of fossil fuels such as coal, oil, and natural gas. It is also emitted during certain industrial processes like cement production. CO_2 has a long atmospheric lifetime, making it a significant contributor to long-term climate change.

Methane (CH_4)
Methane is a potent GHG with a global warming potential (GWP) much higher than CO_2, although it has a shorter atmospheric lifetime. It is released during the production and transport of coal, oil, and natural gas, as well as from livestock and other agricultural practices.

Nitrous Oxide (N_2O)
N_2O is emitted from agricultural and industrial activities, as well as during the combustion of fossil fuels and solid waste. It has a GWP significantly higher than CO_2, making it a critical target for emission reduction efforts, particularly in sectors like agriculture and transportation.

Fluorinated Gases
Fluorinated gases, including hydrofluorocarbons (HFCs), perfluorocarbons (PFCs), sulfur hexafluoride (SF_6), and nitrogen trifluoride (NF_3), are synthetic GHGs used in a variety of industrial applications. These gases have extremely high GWPs, and although they are released in smaller quantities, their impact on climate change is disproportionate.

Regulatory and Voluntary Reporting Frameworks

To effectively manage and reduce emissions, organizations must adhere to various regulatory and voluntary reporting frameworks. These frameworks provide guidelines and standards for measuring, reporting, and verifying emissions.

The Greenhouse Gas Protocol
The GHG Protocol is a widely used international accounting tool for

government and business leaders to understand, quantify, and manage GHG emissions. It provides comprehensive frameworks for measuring and managing emissions from both direct and indirect sources.

International Standards Organization (ISO) 14064
ISO 14064 is a set of standards that provide organizations with a framework for quantifying, monitoring, reporting, and verifying GHG emissions. It includes specific guidelines for the design and implementation of GHG inventories and reduction projects.

Carbon Disclosure Project (CDP)
The CDP is a global disclosure system that enables companies, cities, states, and regions to measure and manage their environmental impacts. Through the CDP, organizations can report their GHG emissions and climate-related strategies, contributing to greater transparency and accountability.

Science-Based Targets Initiative (SBTi)
The SBTi helps companies set ambitious and meaningful corporate GHG reduction targets in line with the latest climate science. By aligning their targets with the Paris Agreement's goal of limiting global warming to well below 2 degrees Celsius, organizations can demonstrate leadership in climate action.

Strategies for Reducing Emissions

Effective emission reduction strategies require a comprehensive understanding of the different types of emissions and their sources. Organizations can adopt various approaches to minimize their carbon footprint, from improving energy efficiency to investing in renewable energy.

Energy Efficiency Improvements
One of the most effective ways to reduce emissions is by improving energy efficiency across all operations. This can involve upgrading equipment, optimizing processes, and implementing energy management systems. Energy audits can help identify areas where efficiency can be enhanced, leading to significant reductions in energy consumption and associated emissions.

Transition to Renewable Energy
Switching to renewable energy sources such as wind, solar, and hydroelectric power can drastically reduce an organization's Scope 2 emissions. Many companies are now investing in on-site renewable energy generation or purchasing renewable energy credits (RECs) to offset their electricity

consumption.

Carbon Offset Programs

Carbon offset programs allow organizations to compensate for their emissions by investing in projects that reduce or remove GHGs from the atmosphere. This can include reforestation, renewable energy projects, and methane capture initiatives. While offsets should not replace direct emission reduction efforts, they can complement a comprehensive climate strategy.

Supply Chain Management

Engaging with suppliers to improve their environmental performance can help reduce Scope 3 emissions. This can involve setting sustainability criteria for supplier selection, collaborating on emission reduction projects, and encouraging the adoption of best practices across the supply chain.

Employee Engagement and Education

Educating and engaging employees in sustainability initiatives is critical for achieving emission reduction goals. Organizations can provide training on energy-efficient practices, encourage the use of public transportation or carpooling, and promote a culture of environmental responsibility.

Innovation and Technology

Investing in innovative technologies can provide new opportunities for emission reductions. This can include advancements in energy storage, carbon capture and storage (CCS), and the development of low-emission products and services. Staying abreast of emerging technologies and integrating them into business operations can yield significant environmental benefits.

In conclusion, understanding the different types of emissions is the first step towards developing effective strategies for their reduction. By categorizing emissions into Scope 1, Scope 2, and Scope 3, and recognizing the specific greenhouse gases involved, organizations can tailor their approaches to address the unique challenges and opportunities they face.

Adhering to regulatory and voluntary reporting frameworks, and adopting a range of reduction strategies, can position companies as leaders in the transition to a sustainable, low-carbon economy.

3.2 Setting Emission Reduction Goals: The Blueprint for a Sustainable Future

In the journey towards a greener, more sustainable future, setting clear and actionable emission reduction goals is paramount. Emissions reduction goals act as the foundation upon which all other sustainability efforts and projects can be built. They provide a strategic direction, measurable targets, and a sense of accountability. This section looks at the intricacies and nuances of setting effective emission reduction goals, ensuring that they are both ambitious and achievable.

Understanding the Importance of Emission Reduction Goals

Emission reduction goals are more than just numbers on a page; they represent a commitment, by top management and the rank and file in an organisation alike, to environmental stewardship and corporate responsibility. These goals are essential for several reasons:

- Regulatory Compliance: Many countries and regions have stringent regulations regarding greenhouse gas emissions. Setting reduction goals helps organizations stay ahead of these regulations and avoid potential fines or sanctions.
- Market Positioning: In today's eco-conscious market, consumers and investors are increasingly allocating resources and capital to companies that demonstrate a commitment to sustainability. Sensible and verifiable emissions reduction goals can enhance a company's reputation and market position.
- Operational Efficiency: Reducing emissions often involves improving energy efficiency, which can lead to significant cost savings in the long run.
- Risk Mitigation: Climate change poses various risks to businesses, including supply chain disruptions and resource scarcity. Emissions reduction goals help mitigate these risks by promoting sustainable practices.

Establishing a Baseline

Before setting emission reduction goals, it is crucial to establish a baseline. The baseline represents the current state of emissions and serves as a reference point for measuring progress. To establish a baseline:

1. Conduct a Comprehensive Emissions Audit: Gather data on all sources of

greenhouse gas emissions within the organization. This includes direct emissions (Scope 1), indirect emissions from purchased electricity (Scope 2), and other indirect emissions (Scope 3) such as those from supply chains and business travel.
2. Utilize Standardized Methodologies: Use standardized methodologies, such as the Greenhouse Gas Protocol, to ensure consistency and accuracy in data collection and reporting.
3. Engage Stakeholders: Involve key stakeholders, including employees, suppliers, and customers, in the data collection process. Their insights and cooperation are invaluable in obtaining accurate data.

Setting SMART Goals

Once the baseline is established, the next step is to set SMART goals—Specific, Measurable, Achievable, Relevant, and Time-bound. Let's break down each component:

- Specific: Goals should be clear and precise, leaving no room for ambiguity. For example, instead of stating, "Reduce emissions," a specific goal would be, "Reduce Scope 1 emissions by 20% by 2025."
- Measurable: Goals must be quantifiable to track progress effectively. Utilize key performance indicators (KPIs) such as carbon footprint reduction, energy consumption per unit of output, and percentage reduction in specific emission sources.
- Achievable: While goals should be ambitious, they must also be realistic and attainable given the organization's resources and constraints. Conduct a feasibility analysis to ensure the goals are achievable and indeed verifiable.
- Relevant: Goals should align with the organization's overall mission and sustainability strategy. They should address the most significant sources of emissions based on the audit and have a meaningful impact on the organization's environmental footprint.
- Time-bound: Set a specific timeframe for achieving the goals. This creates a sense of urgency and accountability. For example, "Achieve a 30% reduction in Scope 2 emissions by 2030."

Engaging Leadership and Gaining Commitment

Setting emission reduction goals requires strong leadership, commitment and communications to and from the top. Without this, sustainability initiatives will, almost certainly, falter. Here are strategies to engage leadership and gain their commitment:

- Present a Compelling Business Case: Highlight the financial, operational, and reputational benefits of reducing emissions. Use data and case studies to demonstrate the potential return on investment.
- Align with existing Corporate Strategy: Ensure that emission reduction goals are integrated into the broader corporate strategy. This alignment underscores the importance of sustainability and ensures that it is prioritized at all levels of the organization.
- Establish Accountability Mechanisms: Assign clear roles and responsibilities for achieving emission reduction goals. Incorporate these goals into performance evaluations and incentive structures.
- Foster a Culture of Sustainability: Promote a culture where sustainability is valued, celebrated and rewarded. Recognize and reward employees and teams that contribute to emission reduction efforts.

Developing an Action Plan

Once goals are set and leadership commitment is secured, the next step is to develop a detailed action plan. This plan should ideally outline the specific steps and initiatives required to achieve the emission reduction goals and include:

- Identifying Key Initiatives and Priorities: Determine the specific projects and initiatives that will drive emission reductions. This may include energy efficiency upgrades, renewable energy investments, process optimization, and supply chain improvements.
- Allocating Resources: Ensure that adequate resources—financial, human, and technical—are allocated to support the initiatives. This may involve securing funding, hiring specialized staff, or investing in new technologies.
- Setting Milestones, Metrics and Deadlines: Break down the goals into smaller, manageable milestones with specific deadlines. This helps maintain momentum and allows for regular progress assessments. What does success look like?
- Monitoring and Reporting: Establish a system for monitoring progress and reporting results. Use tools such as carbon accounting software and sustainability dashboards to track emissions and measure results.
- Continuous Improvement: Embrace a culture of continuous improvement by regularly reviewing and updating the action plan. This

ensures that the organization remains agile and can adapt to new challenges and opportunities.

Leveraging Technology and Innovation

Technology and innovation play a crucial role in achieving emission reduction goals and organizations should leverage the latest advancements to enhance their sustainability efforts:

- Energy Management Systems (EMS): Implement EMS to monitor and control energy consumption in real time. These systems provide valuable insights into energy usage patterns and identify opportunities for efficiency improvements.
- Renewable Energy Solutions: Invest in renewable energy sources such as solar, wind, and geothermal. Explore options for on-site generation and power purchase agreements (PPAs) with renewable energy providers.
- Advanced Analytics and AI: Utilize advanced analytics and artificial intelligence to optimize processes and reduce emissions. Predictive analytics can identify potential issues before they occur, while AI-driven automation can enhance operational efficiency.
- Green Building Technologies: Incorporate green building technologies and practices in new constructions and retrofits. This includes energy-efficient lighting, HVAC systems, and building materials with low environmental impact.
- Innovative Transportation Solutions: Explore innovative transportation solutions such as electric vehicles, telecommuting, and optimized logistics. Reducing transportation-related emissions is a significant component of overall emission reduction efforts.

Collaborating with Stakeholders

Achieving emission reduction goals requires collaboration with a wide range of stakeholders, both internal and external. Effective stakeholder engagement ensures that initiatives are well-supported and that diverse perspectives are considered:

- Internal Stakeholders: Engage employees across all levels of the organization. Foster a sense of ownership and encourage innovative ideas for emission reduction. Provide training and resources to empower employees to contribute to sustainability efforts.
- Suppliers and Partners: Work closely with suppliers and partners to reduce emissions across the supply chain. Establish sustainability criteria for supplier selection and collaborate on joint initiatives to enhance

efficiency and reduce emissions.
- Customers and Communities: Involve customers and communities in sustainability efforts. Educate them about the organization's commitment to emission reduction and encourage their participation. This can enhance brand loyalty and strengthen community relationships.
- Industry Networks and Alliances: Participate in industry networks and alliances focused on sustainability. These platforms provide opportunities for knowledge sharing, collaboration, and advocacy on broader environmental issues.

Overcoming Challenges and Barriers

As always when dealing with humans, change can encounter resistance, if only for its own sake. Setting and achieving emission reduction goals is not without its challenges. Organizations may encounter various barriers, including:

- Financial Constraints: Implementing emission reduction initiatives often requires significant upfront investment. Organizations must explore funding options such as grants, incentives, and green bonds to overcome financial barriers.
- Technological Limitations: Access to advanced technologies may be limited by cost or availability. Organizations should stay informed about emerging technologies and explore partnerships with technology providers.
- Regulatory and Policy Uncertainty: Regulatory and policy changes can create uncertainty and impact emission reduction efforts. Organizations must stay abreast of regulatory developments and advocate for supportive policies.
- Behavioural Resistance: Resistance to change is a common barrier. Organizations should focus on change management strategies, including clear communication, stakeholder engagement, and incentives for behaviour change.
- Data Challenges: Accurate and relevant or mission-critical data collection and reporting are critical for tracking progress. Organizations should invest in robust data management systems and ensure data quality and transparency.

Celebrating Success and Sharing Progress

Recognizing and celebrating successes is essential to maintain momentum and motivation. Organizations should regularly share progress updates and celebrate milestones:

- Public Reporting: Publish annual sustainability reports that highlight progress towards emission reduction goals. These reports should be transparent and provide detailed information on initiatives, achievements, and future plans.
- Internal Communications: Use internal communication channels to share success stories and recognize the contributions of employees and teams. This fosters a sense of pride and ownership in sustainability efforts.
- Awards and Recognition: Apply for sustainability awards and certifications to gain external recognition for emission reduction achievements. This enhances the organization's reputation and motivates continued efforts.
- Continuous Learning and Improvement: Encourage a culture of continuous learning and improvement by regularly reviewing and updating emission reduction strategies. Stay informed about best practices and emerging trends to ensure ongoing success.

To conclude this section, setting emission reduction goals is a critical step in the journey towards a sustainable future. By establishing a clear baseline, setting SMART goals, engaging leadership, developing a detailed action plan, leveraging technology, collaborating with stakeholders, overcoming challenges, and celebrating successes, organizations can achieve significant progress in reducing their environmental footprint. The commitment to emission reduction not only benefits the environment but also enhances operational efficiency, market positioning, and long-term resilience. As we move forward into the 2020s, the importance of setting and achieving ambitious emission reduction goals cannot be overstated. It is a testament to an organization's dedication to sustainability and a brighter, greener future for all.

3.3 Implementing Green Technologies and Practices

In the race against climate change, the implementation of green technologies and practices stands as one of the most critical strategies for reducing emissions. This section explores the great and growing variety of technologies and practices available in this rapidly developing sector today.

By understanding and utilizing these tools, managers can significantly reduce their organizations' carbon footprints while also potentially realizing cost savings and operational efficiencies.

Understanding Green Technologies

Green technologies, also known as clean technologies, encompass a wide range of innovations designed to mitigate the environmental impact of human activities. These technologies are developed with the primary goals of reducing greenhouse gas emissions, conserving energy, and minimizing waste. Key green technologies include renewable energy sources, energy-efficient systems, and waste management solutions.

<u>Renewable Energy Sources</u>
Renewable energy sources, such as solar, wind, hydro, and geothermal power, are pivotal in the transition to a low-carbon economy. These sources generate energy without depleting natural resources or emitting significant amounts of greenhouse gases.

- Solar Power: Solar panels convert sunlight into electricity, providing a clean and sustainable energy source. Solar power can be harnessed at various scales, from residential rooftop installations to large solar farms.
- Wind Power: Wind turbines capture kinetic energy from wind and convert it into electricity. Wind power is particularly effective in regions with high wind speeds and can be deployed both onshore and offshore.
- Hydropower: Hydropower generates electricity by harnessing the energy of flowing water. It is one of the oldest and most widely used renewable energy sources, with applications ranging from small-scale hydroelectric plants to large dams.
- Geothermal Energy: Geothermal energy exploits the heat from within the Earth to generate electricity and provide heating. This renewable source is reliable and has a minimal environmental footprint.

Energy-Efficient Systems
Energy efficiency involves using less energy to perform the same tasks, thereby reducing energy waste. Implementing energy-efficient systems can lead to significant reductions in emissions and operational costs.

- LED Lighting: LED lights are far more energy-efficient than traditional incandescent bulbs, using up to 80% less energy and lasting significantly longer.
- Energy-Efficient HVAC Systems: Modern heating, ventilation, and air conditioning (HVAC) systems are designed to optimize energy use while maintaining comfort levels. These systems often include smart thermostats and advanced controls.
- Building Insulation: Proper insulation reduces the need for heating and cooling by maintaining a stable indoor temperature. High-quality insulation materials and techniques can greatly enhance a building's energy efficiency.
- Energy Management Systems (EMS): EMS provides real-time monitoring and control of energy use within a facility. By analyzing energy consumption patterns, these systems help identify inefficiencies and opportunities for improvement.

Waste Management Solutions
Effective waste management practices minimize the environmental impact of waste production and disposal.

- Recycling and Composting: Recycling reduces the need for raw materials and lowers emissions associated with production processes. Composting organic waste reduces methane emissions from landfills and produces valuable soil amendments.
- Waste-to-Energy (WtE) Technologies: WtE technologies convert waste materials into energy, typically through combustion or anaerobic digestion. These technologies provide a dual benefit of waste reduction and energy generation.
- Sustainable Packaging: Reducing packaging waste through the use of biodegradable, recyclable, or reusable materials helps diminish the environmental footprint of products.

Best Practices for Implementation
Implementing green technologies and practices requires a strategic approach

that encompasses planning, stakeholder engagement, and continuous improvement. The following best practices provide a roadmap for successful implementation:

Conducting a Feasibility Study

Before adopting any green technology or practice, it is essential to conduct a feasibility study to assess its viability and potential impact. This study should evaluate factors such as cost, scalability, and compatibility with existing systems.

Key steps in conducting a feasibility study include:

1. Defining Objectives: Clearly outline the goals of the project, such as reducing emissions, cutting costs, or enhancing sustainability.
2. Analysing Current Practices: Assess the organization's current energy use, waste production, and operational practices to identify areas for improvement. –
3. Technologies Research: Investigate available green technologies and practices, considering their effectiveness, reliability, and alignment with organizational objectives.
4. Cost-Benefit Analysis: Evaluate the financial implications of adopting new technologies, including initial investments, operational costs, and potential savings.
5. Risk Assessment: Identify potential risks associated with the implementation, such as technological failures, regulatory changes, or stakeholder resistance.

Engaging Stakeholders

Successful implementation of green technologies and practices requires the support and involvement of various stakeholders, including employees, management, customers, and suppliers. Engagement strategies include:

- Communication and Education: Inform stakeholders about the benefits and importance of green technologies and practices. Provide training and resources to help them understand their roles in the implementation process.
- Involving Employees: Encourage employee participation by creating green teams or committees tasked with identifying and promoting sustainability initiatives.
- Collaborating with Suppliers: Work with suppliers to source sustainable materials and products, and encourage them to adopt green practices.

- Customer Engagement: Communicate the organization's commitment to sustainability to customers, and highlight the environmental benefits of the products or services offered.

Developing an Implementation Plan

A detailed implementation plan outlines the steps, timelines, and responsibilities for adopting green technologies and practices. To be successful, key components of an implementation plan might include:

1. Project Timeline: Establish a realistic timeline for the implementation, that is aligned with the goals set following previous audits and includes key milestones and deadlines.
2. Resource Allocation: Determine the resources required for the project, including financial, human, and technological assets.
3. Roles and Responsibilities: Assign specific tasks and responsibilities to team members, ensuring accountability and clarity.
4. Monitoring and Evaluation: Develop a system for tracking progress and evaluating the effectiveness of the implemented technologies and practices. Regularly review performance data and make adjustments as needed.

Overcoming Challenges

Implementing green technologies and practices can present several challenges, including financial constraints, technological barriers, and resistance to change. Strategies for overcoming these challenges include:

- Securing Funding: Explore various funding options, such as government grants, subsidies, and incentives, to offset the costs of implementation. Consider all options including partnerships with other organizations or investors.
- Technology Integration: Ensure compatibility between new and existing technologies, and scheduled obsolescence which through careful planning and consultation with experts. Invest in training and support to facilitate a smooth transition.
- Change Management: Address resistance to change by fostering a culture of sustainability and constant process improvement within the organization. Communicate the long-term benefits of green practices and involve employees in decision-making processes.

Case Studies and Success Stories

Learning from the experiences of other organizations can provide valuable insights and inspiration for implementing green technologies and practices. The following case studies highlight successful examples of emission reduction through innovative solutions.

Solar Power Adoption in a Manufacturing Facility
A leading manufacturing company in the automotive industry sought to reduce its carbon footprint by adopting solar power. The company conducted a feasibility study to assess the potential impact and cost savings of installing solar panels on its production facility. The study revealed that solar power could meet 30% of the facility's energy needs, resulting in substantial emissions reductions and cost savings.

After securing funding through government subsidies and incentives, the company installed a 5 MW solar array on its facility's rooftop. The project was completed within six months, and the solar panels began generating electricity immediately. The company also implemented an energy management system to monitor and optimize energy use. The results were impressive and the company reduced its annual greenhouse gas emissions by some 10,000 metric tons and achieved significant energy cost savings.

The success of the solar power project inspired the company to pursue additional sustainability initiatives, including energy-efficient lighting and waste reduction programs.

Energy-Efficient HVAC Systems in a Commercial Office Building
A commercial real estate firm aimed to enhance the energy efficiency of one of its flagship office buildings. The building's outdated HVAC system was identified as a major source of peak and off-peak energy waste and high operating costs. The firm decided to upgrade to a modern, energy-efficient HVAC system with advanced controls and smart thermostats.

The implementation plan included conducting a thorough energy audit, selecting the appropriate HVAC system, and engaging stakeholders in the process. The firm also invested in employee training to ensure proper operation and maintenance of the new system.

The upgraded HVAC system resulted in a 25% reduction in energy use and a significant decrease in operating costs. The building's tenants reported improved comfort levels, and the firm received positive feedback for its commitment to sustainability.

The success of the project led the firm to implement similar upgrades in other properties within its portfolio.

Waste-to-Energy Technology in a Municipal Waste Management Program
A municipal government sought to address the growing issue of waste management and reduce landfill use. The municipality decided to invest in waste-to-energy (WtE) technology to convert organic waste into biogas, which could be used to generate electricity and heat.

The implementation process involved conducting a feasibility study, securing funding, and selecting the appropriate WtE technology. The municipality collaborated with local waste management companies and engaged residents through public education campaigns. The WtE facility successfully diverted significant organic waste from landfills and generated renewable energy to power municipal buildings. The project reduced greenhouse gas emissions by 15,000 metric tons annually and contributed to the municipality's sustainability goals. The success of the WtE program garnered national recognition and served as a model for other cities.

Implementing green technologies and practices is crucial to reducing emissions and achieving sustainability goals. Managers can successfully integrate these solutions into their organisations by understanding the available technologies, conducting thorough feasibility studies, engaging stakeholders, and developing detailed implementation plans. The case studies presented in this section demonstrate the tangible benefits of green technologies, from cost savings to emissions reductions.

3.4 Emissions Monitoring and Reporting: The Cornerstones of Sustainable Management

In this rapidly evolving corporate landscape that we now live in, the importance of monitoring and reporting emission levels cannot be overstated. As organizations strive to minimize their environmental footprint, a structured approach to emissions monitoring and reporting becomes indispensable.

In this section we will observe some of the nuances of establishing robust monitoring systems, leveraging cutting-edge technology, and adhering to best practices in reporting emissions. The purpose of these tools and practices is to effectively oversee the organization's emissions, ensuring transparency, compliance, and continuous improvement in your sustainability initiatives.

The Importance of Emissions Monitoring

As discussed previously in this chapter emissions monitoring is the process of systematically measuring the amount of pollutants released into the atmosphere by an organization. Effective emissions monitoring serves multiple purposes:

1. Regulatory Compliance: Many regions have stringent regulations governing emissions. Monitoring ensures that your organization remains compliant with local, national, and international laws.
2. Environmental Impact: Understanding your emissions helps gauge your environmental footprint and identify areas for improvement.
3. Reputation Management: Demonstrating a commitment to reducing emissions can enhance your organization's reputation among stakeholders, including customers, investors, and employees.
4. Cost Savings: Identifying and mitigating emissions can lead to increased operational efficiency and cost savings.

Establishing an Emissions Monitoring System

Setting up an emissions monitoring system involves several critical steps:

<u>Define Objectives and Scope</u>
Before implementing a monitoring system, it's essential to clearly define the objectives and scope of the monitoring. Consider the following questions:

- What types of emissions will be monitored?
- Which facilities or operations will be included?

- What are the regulatory requirements?
- What are the internal sustainability goals?

Select Appropriate Monitoring Methods

Depending on the type of emissions and the specific requirements of your organization, different monitoring methods may be employed:

- Direct Monitoring: Continuous Emission Monitoring Systems (CEMS) are used to provide real-time data on emissions. These systems are typically installed on stacks or vents.
- Indirect Monitoring: Emissions can also be estimated based on fuel consumption, production rates, or other activity data. This method often involves using emission factors.

Implement Data Collection and Management Systems

Robust data collection and management systems are essential for accurate emissions monitoring. Key components include:

- Sensors and Instruments: High-quality sensors and instruments should be installed to collect real-time data.
- Data Management Software: Use software to collect, store, and analyze emissions data. Ensure the software can handle large datasets and provide detailed reports.
- Integration with Existing Systems: Emissions monitoring systems should be integrated with existing operational and environmental management systems for seamless data flow.

Leveraging Technology for Emissions Monitoring

Technological advancements have revolutionized emissions monitoring, making it more accurate and efficient. Some cutting-edge technologies include:

Internet of Things (IoT) Devices

IoT devices can be deployed to monitor emissions in real-time. These devices collect data from various sources and transmit it to a central system for analysis. Benefits of IoT in emissions monitoring include:

- Real-time data collection and analysis
- Remote monitoring capabilities
- Enhanced accuracy and reliability

Artificial Intelligence (AI) and Machine Learning (ML)
AI and ML algorithms can analyze vast amounts of emissions data to identify patterns and predict future trends. These technologies can also help optimize emissions reduction strategies by providing actionable insights.

Blockchain Technology
Blockchain can be used to enhance the transparency and integrity of emissions data. By creating an immutable ledger, blockchain ensures that emissions data is accurate and tamper-proof.

Best Practices in Emissions Reporting

Accurate and transparent reporting of emissions is crucial for demonstrating accountability and compliance. Here are some best practices to consider:

Adopt Standardized Reporting Frameworks
Several standardized frameworks are available for emissions reporting, including:

- The Greenhouse Gas Protocol: A widely used framework for measuring and managing GHG emissions.
- ISO 14064: An international standard that provides guidelines for the quantification and reporting of GHG emissions.
- CDP Reporting: A global disclosure system for managing environmental impacts.

Adopting these frameworks ensures consistency and comparability of emissions data.

Ensure Data Accuracy and Transparency
Accurate and transparent data is the cornerstone of credible emissions reporting. To achieve this:

- Conduct Regular Audits: Regularly audit your emissions data to identify and correct any discrepancies.
- Use Verified Data Sources: Ensure that data is sourced from verified and reliable instruments and systems.
- Provide Detailed Disclosures: Include detailed disclosures in your reports, outlining the methodologies and assumptions used in data collection and analysis.

Engage Stakeholders
Engaging stakeholders in the emissions reporting process is essential for building trust and credibility.

- Internal Engagement: Involve employees at all levels in the monitoring and reporting process. Provide training and resources to help them understand the importance of emissions management.
- External Engagement: Communicate your emissions data and reduction efforts to external stakeholders, including customers, investors, and regulatory bodies. Use multiple channels, such as annual reports, sustainability reports, and social media.

Case Studies: Successful Emissions Monitoring and Reporting

To provide a practical perspective, let's explore some case studies of organizations that have successfully implemented emissions monitoring and reporting systems:

1. Case Study: ABC Manufacturing
ABC Manufacturing, a leading producer of consumer goods, faced increasing pressure from stakeholders to reduce its environmental impact. The company implemented a comprehensive emissions monitoring system, which included:

Installation of CEMS: Continuous Emission Monitoring Systems were installed at key production facilities to provide real-time data on CO_2 and NO_x emissions.

Integration with IoT: IoT devices were deployed to monitor emissions from various sources, including boilers, furnaces, and vehicles.

Data Management Software: A centralized software platform was used to collect, store, and analyse emissions data. The platform provided detailed, formatted and branded reports, and online dashboards for management review.

As a result, ABC Manufacturing achieved an almost 15% reduction in CO_2 emissions within the first year of implementation. The company also gained recognition for its sustainability efforts and improved employee retention because of its initiatives.

2. Case Study: XYZ Energy
XYZ Energy, a renewable energy provider, aimed to enhance its own

emissions reporting to meet regulatory requirements and attract environmentally conscious investors. The company adopted the following strategies:

- Standardized Reporting Framework: XYZ Energy adopted the Greenhouse Gas Protocol and ISO 14064 standards for emissions reporting.
- Stakeholder Engagement: The company engaged stakeholders through regular sustainability reports, webinars, and social media updates.

Longer term, the company is also looking into the possibility of using developing blockchain technologies to create an immutable ledger of emissions data, ensuring transparency and integrity and possibly work with carbon credits.

XYZ Energy's emissions reporting initiative resulted in increased investor confidence and improved compliance with regulatory requirements. The company also received positive feedback from various stakeholders.

Overcoming Challenges in Emissions Monitoring and Reporting

Despite the benefits, emissions monitoring and reporting can present several challenges. Here are some common challenges and strategies to overcome them:

Data Accuracy and Quality
Ensuring the accuracy and quality of emissions data can be challenging due to factors such as equipment malfunctions, human error, and inconsistent data sources. To address these challenges:

- Regular Calibration and Maintenance: Regularly calibrate and maintain monitoring equipment to ensure accurate data collection.
- Training and Education: Provide training to employees on proper data collection and reporting procedures.
- Use of Redundant Systems: Implement redundant systems to cross-verify data and identify discrepancies.

Complexity of Regulations
Navigating the complex landscape of emissions regulations can be daunting. To manage regulatory complexity:

- Stay Informed: Keep abreast of regulatory changes and updates at local, national, and international levels.
- Consult Experts: Engage with regulatory experts and consultants to ensure compliance with relevant laws and standards.
- Utilize Software Solutions: Leverage software solutions that can help track regulatory requirements and automate compliance reporting.

Resource Constraints
Implementing and maintaining an emissions monitoring and reporting system can be resource-intensive. Resource constraints can be addressed as follows:

- Prioritize Key Areas: Focus on monitoring and reporting emissions from key sources that have the most significant impact.
- Seek External Funding: Explore funding opportunities from government grants, subsidies, and environmental organizations.
- Collaborate with Partners: Collaborate with industry partners, research institutions, and NGOs to share resources and expertise.

The Future of Emissions Monitoring and Reporting
As technology continues to evolve, the future of emissions monitoring and reporting holds exciting possibilities. Here are some trends to watch:

Advanced Sensor Technology
Emerging sensor technologies, such as nanotechnology and biosensors, promise to enhance the accuracy and sensitivity of emissions monitoring. These advancements will enable more precise measurements of pollutants and facilitate real-time monitoring.

Integration with Environmental Management Systems (EMS)
Integrating emissions monitoring with comprehensive EMS will provide a holistic view of an organization's environmental performance. This integration will streamline data management, reporting, and decision-making processes.

Increased Use of Predictive Analytics
Predictive analytics, powered by AI and ML, will play a more prominent role in emissions management. These tools will enable organizations to anticipate emissions trends, optimize reduction strategies, and proactively address potential issues.

To conclude, the monitoring and reporting of emissions is a fundamental component of sustainable management. By establishing robust monitoring systems, leveraging advanced technologies, and adhering to best practices in reporting, organisations can effectively manage their emissions, ensure compliance, and demonstrate their commitment to environmental stewardship.

3.5 Unlocking Financial Support: Government Incentives and Grants for Emission Reduction

One of the most substantial barriers businesses encounter can be the financial resources or investment funding required for implementing emission reduction strategies. While the long-term benefits of reducing emissions may be clear and include lowered operational costs, enhanced brand reputation, and compliance with regulatory requirements - the initial costs can be daunting.

Fortunately, governments worldwide recognize the importance of supporting businesses in their transition to sustainable practices. As a result, they often offer various incentives and grants designed to alleviate the financial burden and encourage more organizations to take proactive steps in reducing their carbon footprint.

This section explores the myriad of government incentives and grants available, providing a roadmap for managers to navigate and leverage these resources effectively.

Understanding Government Incentives

Government incentives come in many forms, from direct grants and tax credits to low-interest loans and rebates. Understanding the types of incentives available can help busiess owners and managers identify the most beneficial options for their specific needs.

Direct Grants

Direct grants are funds provided by the government that do not need to be repaid. These grants are often competitive, requiring businesses to apply and demonstrate their commitment to emission reduction through detailed proposals and plans. Examples of direct grants in the US include, but each jurisdiction will have something similar:

- The Climate Action Fund (CAF): Available in many countries, CAF provides financial support to projects that significantly reduce greenhouse gas emissions. Businesses can apply for grants to cover costs associated with new technologies, energy-efficient upgrades, and other emission reduction measures.
- The Green Business Fund: This fund offers grants to small and medium-sized enterprises (SMEs) for energy efficiency audits, equipment upgrades, and employee training related to emission reduction.

Tax Credits and Deductions

Tax credits and deductions reduce the amount of tax a business owes, effectively providing financial relief for investments in emission reduction initiatives. Notable examples include:

- The Investment Tax Credit (ITC): This credit allows businesses to deduct a significant percentage of the cost of installing renewable energy systems, such as solar panels or wind turbines, from their federal taxes.
- Accelerated Depreciation: Under this incentive, businesses can depreciate the cost of energy-efficient equipment more quickly, allowing them to recover their investment sooner through reduced tax liability.

Low-Interest Loans and Rebates

Low-interest loans and rebates provide financial assistance for businesses to invest in emission-reduction technologies and practices. These incentives help reduce the upfront costs and make sustainable investments more accessible. Examples include:

- The Green Loan Program: This program offers low-interest loans to businesses for projects that improve energy efficiency and reduce emissions. The loans can be used for a variety of purposes, including upgrading HVAC systems, installing energy-efficient lighting, and retrofitting buildings.
- Energy Efficiency Rebates: Many utility companies offer rebates to businesses that implement energy-saving measures. These rebates can significantly offset the costs of new equipment and technologies.

Navigating the Application Process

Securing government incentives often requires navigating a complex application process. Here are some key steps to consider:

Research and Identify Relevant Programs

The first step is to research and identify the government programs and incentives that are relevant to your business and its emission reduction goals. This involves:

- Reviewing Government Websites: Visit the websites of relevant government agencies, such as the Department of Energy, Environmental Protection Agency, and local energy offices, to find information on available incentives.

- Consulting Industry Associations: Industry associations often provide resources and guidance on available incentives. They can also connect you with other businesses that have successfully secured funding.

Prepare a Comprehensive Proposal
Once you have identified the relevant programs, the next step is to prepare a comprehensive proposal. This proposal should include:

1. A Detailed Project Plan: Outline the specific emission reduction measures you plan to implement, including timelines, costs, and expected outcomes.
2. Evidence of Impact: Provide data and analysis to demonstrate the potential impact of your project on reducing emissions. This can include projected energy savings, reduced greenhouse gas emissions, and other environmental benefits.
3. Financial Projections: Include detailed financial projections that show the expected return on investment and how the funding will be used.

Submit the Application
After preparing your proposal, apply according to the program's guidelines. Be sure to:

- Follow Submission Guidelines: Carefully follow the submission guidelines provided by the funding agency. This includes meeting deadlines, providing all required documentation, and adhering to formatting requirements.
- Seek Feedback: If possible, seek feedback on your proposal from colleagues or industry experts before submitting it. This can help identify any areas for improvement and increase your chances of success.

Maximizing the Benefits of Government Incentives

Once you have secured government incentives, it is essential to maximize their benefits by implementing best practices in project management and monitoring.

Effective Project Management
Effective project management is critical to the successful implementation of emission reduction initiatives. This includes:

- Setting Clear Goals and Milestones: Establish clear goals and milestones for your project to ensure it stays on track. This includes setting specific, measurable, achievable, relevant, and time-bound (SMART) objectives.

- Regular Monitoring and Reporting: Regularly monitor and report on the progress of your project. This includes tracking key performance indicators (KPIs), such as energy savings and emission reductions, and providing updates to stakeholders.
- Adapting to Changes: Be prepared to adapt to changes and challenges that may arise during the implementation of your project. This includes adjusting timelines, budgets, and strategies as needed.

Continuous Improvement
Continuous improvement is essential to sustaining the benefits of emission reduction initiatives. This includes:

- Ongoing Training and Education: Provide ongoing training and education to employees on best practices for energy efficiency and emission reduction. This can help ensure that your team remains engaged and committed to your sustainability goals.
- Regular Audits and Assessments: Conduct regular audits and assessments to identify new opportunities for improvement. This includes reviewing energy usage data, conducting site inspections, and seeking feedback from employees and stakeholders.
- Leveraging New Technologies: Stay informed about new technologies and innovations in the field of emission reduction. This includes attending industry conferences, participating in webinars, and networking with other professionals.

Case Studies: Success Stories of Government Incentive Utilization

To illustrate the impact of government incentives on emission reduction, let's explore a few success stories from businesses that have effectively leveraged these resources.

Tech Innovators Inc.
Tech Innovators Inc., a mid-sized technology company, secured a grant from the Climate Action Fund to retrofit their headquarters with energy-efficient lighting and HVAC systems. By implementing these upgrades, the company reduced its energy consumption by 30% and cut its greenhouse gas emissions by 25%. The grant covered 50% of the project costs, making the investment financially viable for the company.

Green Manufacturing Ltd.
Green Manufacturing Ltd., a small manufacturing firm, utilized the Investment Tax Credit to install a solar array on their facility's rooftop. The solar panels now generate 60% of the company's electricity needs, significantly lowering their energy bills and reducing their carbon footprint. The tax credit allowed Green Manufacturing to recover 30% of the installation costs, accelerating their return on investment.

Eco-Friendly Retailers
Eco-Friendly Retailers, a chain of retail stores, took advantage of the Green Loan Program to finance the installation of energy-efficient refrigeration units across their locations. The new units have reduced the stores' energy consumption by 40%, resulting in substantial cost savings. The low-interest loan made the project affordable, and the company expects to see a full return on investment within five years.

Government incentives and grants play a crucial role in helping businesses overcome the financial barriers to emission reduction. By understanding the types of incentives available, navigating the application process, and maximizing the benefits of secured funding, managers can drive their organizations toward a more sustainable future.

As the examples of Tech Innovators Inc., Green Manufacturing Ltd., and Eco-Friendly Retailers demonstrate, leveraging government support can lead to significant environmental and financial gains. Embrace these opportunities and lead your organization on the path to sustainability, ensuring a greener, more prosperous future for all.

3.6 Real-Life Success Stories in Emission Reduction

In this section, we'll explore various real-life examples of individuals and organizations that have successfully implemented strategies to reduce their emissions. These stories not only illustrate the practical steps taken but also highlight the tangible benefits and challenges encountered along the way. Each case study serves as a testament to the impact and feasibility of adopting green technologies and practices.

From Carbon Footprint to Carbon Neutral: The Journey of Patagonia
Patagonia, the renowned outdoor clothing and gear company, has long been a pioneer in environmental responsibility. Their journey towards carbon neutrality offers a compelling case study in emission reduction. Founded in

1973 by Yvon Chouinard, Patagonia has always been committed to sustainability. The company took another significant step forward in 2016 when it announced its goal to become carbon neutral by 2025. This ambitious target involved a multifaceted approach, including energy efficiency, renewable energy adoption, and offsetting unavoidable emissions.

One of the first steps Patagonia took was to conduct a comprehensive audit of its carbon footprint. This audit revealed that the majority of their emissions stemmed from the manufacturing process, particularly in the production of synthetic fibres. Armed with this knowledge, Patagonia shifted its focus to sourcing more sustainable materials, like recycled polyester and organic cotton. They also invested in innovative technologies to reduce emissions during production, such as adopting low-impact dyeing processes.

To further reduce their carbon footprint, Patagonia ramped up its use of renewable energy. By 2020, the company had transitioned to using 100% renewable electricity in its owned and operated facilities. They also partnered with suppliers to encourage the adoption of renewable energy in the manufacturing process. Additionally, Patagonia invested in renewable energy projects, such as wind and solar farms, to offset emissions they couldn't eliminate outright.

A critical component of Patagonia's strategy was its commitment to transparency. The company regularly published detailed reports on its progress towards carbon neutrality, including both successes and setbacks. This openness not only built trust with consumers but also inspired other companies to adopt similar practices. Patagonia's efforts were not without challenges. The transition to more sustainable materials and processes often came with higher costs and required significant investment. However, the company viewed these costs as an investment in the future, both for the planet and for their business.

By positioning the organisation as an environmental leader, Patagonia strengthened its brand loyalty and attracted a growing base of eco-conscious consumers. As of 2023, Patagonia is on track to meet its carbon neutrality goal by 2025. Their journey serves as a powerful example of how a company can successfully implement emission reduction strategies, balancing environmental responsibility with business growth.

Greening the Grid: How Denmark Became a Leader in Renewable Energy

Denmark's transformation into a global leader in renewable energy and emission reduction is a remarkable story of national commitment and innovative policy-making. In the early 1990s, Denmark faced a significant challenge: how to reduce its dependence on fossil fuels and cut greenhouse gas emissions. The country decided to take bold action, setting ambitious goals for renewable energy adoption and emission reduction. By 2020, Denmark aimed to source half of its electricity from wind power and become carbon neutral by 2050.

The Danish government implemented a series of policies and incentives to encourage the development of renewable energy. One of the most successful initiatives was the introduction of feed-in tariffs, which guaranteed fixed payments to renewable energy producers for the electricity they generated. This policy provided the financial certainty needed to spur investment in wind power and other renewable energy sources. Denmark also invested heavily in research and development of renewable technologies. The country became a hub for wind energy innovation, with companies like Vestas and Siemens Gamesa leading the way. These companies developed more efficient and cost-effective wind turbines, which helped drive down the cost of wind power and made it a viable alternative to fossil fuels.

Another key aspect of Denmark's strategy was community involvement. The Danish government encouraged local communities to invest in wind farms, often through cooperative ownership models. This approach not only provided financial benefits to local residents but also fostered widespread public support for renewable energy projects. Denmark's efforts paid off. By 2020, the country had exceeded its goal, with wind power accounting for over 50% of its electricity consumption. The shift to renewable energy significantly reduced Denmark's greenhouse gas emissions, contributing to a broader European effort to combat climate change. One of the most impressive aspects of Denmark's renewable energy transition is its impact on the economy. The renewable energy sector has created thousands of jobs and established Denmark as a leader in green technology exports.

The success of the wind industry, in particular, has positioned Denmark as a key player in the global transition to renewable energy. Denmark's journey to becoming a renewable energy leader demonstrates the power of bold policy-making, innovation, and community involvement. It shows that with the right strategies and commitment, it is possible to significantly reduce emissions and build a sustainable energy future.

Clearing the Air: How New York City Reduced Its Emissions

New York City, one of the world's largest and most densely populated urban areas, has made significant strides in reducing its emissions over the past two decades. The city's comprehensive approach offers valuable lessons for other urban centres grappling with the challenges of climate change.

In 2007, New York City launched PlaNYC, a long-term sustainability plan aimed at reducing greenhouse gas emissions by 30% by 2030. The plan included a wide range of initiatives, from improving energy efficiency in buildings to expanding public transportation and increasing the use of renewable energy. One of the most impactful components of PlaNYC was the Greener, Greater Buildings Plan (GGBP). This initiative targeted the city's largest buildings, which are responsible for the majority of its emissions. The GGBP required energy audits and retro-commissioning for these buildings, as well as mandatory energy efficiency upgrades. Property owners were also required to benchmark their buildings' energy use and publicly disclose the results, promoting transparency and accountability.

To support these efforts, the city offered a variety of incentives and financing options. For example, the NYC Energy Efficiency Corporation (NYCEEC) provided low-cost financing for energy efficiency projects, helping property owners overcome the upfront costs of retrofits.

New York City also focused on increasing the use of renewable energy. The city installed solar panels on public buildings and incentivized the adoption of solar energy in the private sector. Additionally, the city explored innovative solutions like offshore wind farms and energy storage systems to enhance grid reliability and reduce reliance on fossil fuels. Transportation was another key area of focus. The city expanded its public transportation network, introduced bike-sharing programs, and implemented congestion pricing to reduce traffic and emissions. These efforts not only lowered emissions but also improved air quality and quality of life for residents. As a result of these comprehensive efforts, New York City achieved a 15% reduction in greenhouse gas emissions by 2016, putting it on track to meet its 2030 goal.

The city's success demonstrates the effectiveness of a holistic approach that combines regulatory measures, incentives, and public engagement. New York City's experience highlights the importance of leadership and collaboration in tackling climate change. By setting ambitious goals, implementing a diverse array of strategies, and fostering public-private partnerships, the city has made significant progress in reducing its emissions and building a more sustainable future.

Conclusion: Achieving Effective Emission Reductions

In conclusion, reducing emissions is a multifaceted challenge that requires a comprehensive understanding and strategic approach.

By first understanding the different types of emissions, managers can identify the most significant sources and areas for improvement. Setting clear and measurable emission reduction goals is essential for guiding efforts and measuring progress.

Implementing green technologies and practices can offer substantial benefits, both in terms of reduced emissions and operational efficiencies.

Continuous monitoring and reporting of emission levels ensure transparency and accountability, enabling organizations to track their progress and make informed adjustments as needed.

Additionally, leveraging government incentives and grants can provide valuable financial support and enhance the feasibility of ambitious emission reduction projects.

By integrating these strategies, managers can not only contribute to a more sustainable future but also position their organizations as leaders in environmental responsibility.

Remember, the journey towards emission reduction is ongoing, and continuous improvement is key to long-term success.

4 IMPROVEMENT OPPORTUNITIES: ENHANCING EFFICIENCY

Welcome to Chapter 4, where we really get into the heart of operational transformation: identifying and seizing improvement opportunities to enhance efficiency within your organization.

As businesses face mounting pressure from regulatory frameworks, increasing energy costs, and growing consumer demand for sustainability, the ability to pinpoint inefficiencies and transform them into strengths becomes vital to the competitive edge of the modern business.

This chapter serves as your roadmap to uncovering hidden potential within your organization, laying the groundwork for a future where efficiency and sustainability go hand in hand.

We begin by exploring the critical task of identifying and prioritizing improvement areas. This involves a methodical approach to auditing current practices, leveraging data analytics, and utilizing innovative tools to uncover inefficiencies that may not be immediately visible.

By the end of this section, you will have a clear understanding of how to conduct a thorough assessment and develop a prioritized action plan tailored to your unique organizational needs.

Next, we turn our attention to energy-efficient building design and retrofit options. Buildings are often the largest consumers of energy within an organization, and therefore, hold immense potential for improvement. From the integration of cutting-edge technologies to the adoption of smart building systems, we will explore a variety of strategies designed to minimize energy usage while maximizing operational efficiency. Whether you are designing a new facility or retrofitting an existing structure, this section provides practical insights and actionable steps to achieve significant energy savings.

Harnessing the power of renewable energy sources is another critical component of enhancing efficiency. As traditional energy sources become increasingly unsustainable, the shift towards renewables offers not only environmental benefits but also substantial cost savings and energy security. We will guide you through the process of evaluating and implementing renewable energy solutions, from solar and wind to bioenergy and beyond. By integrating these sources into your energy mix, you can reduce your reliance on fossil fuels and create a more resilient energy infrastructure.

However, technological advancements alone are not enough. The role of behavioural changes and employee engagement cannot be overstated. Engaging your workforce in sustainability initiatives is essential for achieving long-term success. This section will provide strategies for fostering a culture of sustainability, encouraging behavioural changes, and ensuring that every member of your organization is aligned with your efficiency goals. From training programs to incentive structures, we will explore various approaches to cultivating an engaged and proactive workforce.

Finally, we address the critical aspect of quantifying the return on investment (ROI) of sustainability initiatives. Measuring the financial benefits of your efficiency efforts is crucial for securing ongoing support and investment. We will discuss the methodologies for calculating ROI, including cost savings, productivity gains, and environmental impact. By presenting a clear and compelling business case, you can demonstrate the value of your sustainability initiatives to stakeholders and ensure the continued success of your green management strategies.

As you navigate through this chapter, remember that improvement opportunities are not just about cutting costs or meeting regulatory requirements. They are about creating a more sustainable, resilient, and forward-thinking organization. By embracing efficiency as a core principle, you can drive innovation, enhance your competitive advantage, and contribute positively to the global sustainability movement.

Let's embark on this journey together and unlock the full potential of improvement opportunities to enhance efficiency within your organization.

4.1 Pinpointing Potential: Identifying and Prioritizing Improvement Areas

Organizations striving for sustainable success must first identify and prioritize areas that offer the most significant opportunities for improvement. This process requires a detailed and systematic approach that ensures no stone is left unturned. By focusing on key areas such as energy consumption, emissions reduction, and overall efficiency, managers can develop a comprehensive plan to enhance their organization's green practices.

Conducting a Comprehensive Energy Audit

As discussed in previous chapters the journey towards identifying improvement areas begins with a thorough energy audit. This audit acts as the diagnostic tool and starting point providing a clear snapshot of current energy use, identifying inefficiencies, and highlighting potential areas for improvement. The energy audit process typically involves the following steps:

- Data Collection - should be standardised across various locations
- Site Inspection - highlights specific location-based anomalies and opportunities
- Analysis and Benchmarking - are used to determine best-in-class metrics and targets.
- Identifying Inefficiencies – these provide the real meat of the audit and serve not to criticise current problems but to identify Improvement Opportunities.
- Reporting and Recommendations – consistency serves the entire organisation across locations and also helps in communicating tasks and targets later.

Prioritizing High-Impact Areas

Once potential improvement areas have been identified, the next step is to prioritize them. Not all opportunities are created equal and will have the same impact on energy efficiency and sustainability, so it is crucial to focus on those that offer the greatest return on investment. Consider the following factors when prioritizing improvement areas:

- Energy Savings Potential: Evaluate the potential energy savings of each identified area. Focus on initiatives that can deliver the more substantial reductions in energy consumption.
- Cost-Effectiveness: Assess the cost of implementing each improvement. Prioritize low-cost, high-impact initiatives to ensure the best use of available resources.
- Ease of Implementation: Consider the complexity and feasibility of implementing each improvement. Prioritize the 'low hanging fruit' and initiatives that can be easily and quickly implemented without significant disruption to operations.
- Regulatory Compliance: Consider whether the prioritized improvement areas align with current regulations and standards. This not only helps in achieving sustainability goals but also ensures legal compliance.
- Long-Term Benefits: Look beyond immediate gains and consider the long-term benefits of each improvement. Prioritize initiatives that offer sustained energy savings, support the organization's long-term sustainability goals or impact the marketing effort, internal or external, positively.

Leveraging Technology for Efficiency

Technology plays a critical role in identifying and prioritizing improvement areas. Advanced tools and software can help organizations analyze energy consumption patterns, simulate the impact of potential improvements, and monitor progress in real-time. Key technologies to consider include:

- Energy Management Systems (EMS): Consistent monitoring and control across different facilities can provide real-time data, and long-term insights enabling managers to identify inefficiencies and make informed decisions.
- Building Automation Systems (BAS): BAS integrates various building systems such as lighting, HVAC, and security, allowing for centralized control and optimization. This can significantly enhance energy efficiency and reduce costs.
- Smart Sensors and IoT Devices: Deploying smart sensors and IoT devices can provide granular insights into energy use. These devices can

detect anomalies, predict maintenance needs, and optimize both energy consumption in real-time, and preventive maintenance programs.
- Data Analytics and AI: Leveraging data analytics and artificial intelligence can help organizations identify patterns and trends in energy use. AI-powered tools can also simulate the impact of potential improvements, enabling more accurate prioritization.

Engaging Stakeholders in the Process

It cannot be over emphasised that identifying and prioritizing improvement areas is not a task for managers alone – it is the people who live with the systems that can identify the anomalies, inefficiencies, risks and opportunities for improvement that exist in every complex system.

Engaging stakeholders from across the organization can provide valuable insights and foster a culture of sustainability. Key steps to engage stakeholders include:

- Form a Green Team: Establish a cross-functional team dedicated to sustainability initiatives. This team should include representatives from different departments, ensuring diverse perspectives and expertise.
- Conducting Periodic Workshops and Training: Organize workshops and training sessions to educate employees about the importance of energy efficiency and sustainability. Provide them with the knowledge and tools needed to contribute to improvement efforts.
- Soliciting Feedback and Ideas: Encourage employees to share their ideas and feedback on potential improvement areas. This can uncover opportunities that may not be evident to management alone.
- Recognizing and Rewarding Contributions: Acknowledge and reward employees who contribute to identifying and implementing improvement areas. This can motivate others to participate and support sustainability initiatives.

Developing an Action Plan with Buy-In

With prioritized improvement areas identified, the next step is to develop a detailed action plan. This plan should outline the steps needed to implement each improvement, assign responsibilities, and establish timelines. Key components of an action plan include:

- Setting Clear Metrics and Objectives: Define specific, measurable

objectives for each improvement area. This provides a clear direction and helps track progress.
- Assigning Responsibilities: Identify individuals or teams responsible for implementing each improvement. Ensure they have the necessary resources and support to succeed.
- Establishing Timelines: Develop a realistic timeline for each improvement initiative. This includes setting milestones and deadlines to ensure timely completion.
- Monitoring and Evaluation: Implement a system to monitor progress and evaluate the effectiveness of each improvement. This allows for adjustments and ensures continuous improvement.
- Communicating Progress: Keep stakeholders informed about the progress of improvement initiatives. Regular updates and transparent communication and feedback all foster engagement and support.

Case Studies and Best Practices

Learning from the experiences of others can provide valuable insights and inspiration. Throughout the previous case studies we say how best practices have successfully identified and prioritized improvement areas. Using your own case study format will highlight the strategies that can be used actoss the organisation, the challenges they faced, and the outcomes they achieved.

Many organizations have found success by actively engaging employees in the process. Forming green teams, conducting workshops, and recognizing contributions have all proven effective in fostering a culture of sustainability.

Identifying and prioritizing improvement areas is a critical step in enhancing energy efficiency and sustainability. By conducting comprehensive energy audits, leveraging technology, engaging stakeholders, and developing detailed action plans, organizations can uncover significant opportunities for improvement. This systematic approach not only helps achieve immediate energy savings but also supports long-term sustainability goals. With the right strategies in place, managers can lead their organizations towards a greener, more efficient future.

4.2 Energy-Efficient Building Design and Retrofit Options

In the quest for sustainability, the design and retrofitting of buildings play a pivotal role. Buildings are among the largest energy consumers, and their efficient design can significantly reduce energy consumption, emissions, and operational costs.

This section delves into the myriad opportunities available for enhancing the energy efficiency of buildings, from new constructions to retrofits of existing structures.

The Foundations of Energy-Efficient Building Design

Energy-efficient building design starts at the conceptual phase. Integrating sustainability principles right from the planning stage ensures that the building's energy footprint is minimized over its lifecycle. Key considerations include site selection, building orientation, and the use of sustainable materials.

Site Selection and Building Orientation
The location and orientation of a building can greatly influence its energy consumption. Selecting a site with optimal solar exposure and natural shading can reduce the need for artificial lighting and climate control. For instance, positioning a building to maximize natural sunlight in colder climates can reduce heating needs, while strategic shading can minimize cooling requirements in warmer regions.

Sustainable Building Materials
The choice of materials is another critical factor. Using locally sourced, recycled, or renewable materials reduces the environmental impact of construction. Materials with high thermal mass, such as concrete or brick, can help regulate indoor temperatures by absorbing and releasing heat slowly. Additionally, the use of low-emissivity (Low-E) windows and reflective roofing materials can further enhance energy efficiency.

Advanced Insulation Techniques
Insulation is a cornerstone of energy-efficient design. Proper insulation minimizes heat transfer, reducing the need for heating and cooling. Advanced insulation materials, such as spray foam, rigid foam boards, and insulated concrete forms, offer superior performance compared to traditional options. Moreover, ensuring that all parts of the building envelope are well-insulated, including walls, roofs, and floors, is crucial for maintaining consistent indoor

temperatures.

Energy-Efficient HVAC Systems

Heating, ventilation, and air conditioning (HVAC) systems are major energy consumers in buildings. Implementing energy-efficient HVAC systems can lead to substantial energy savings. High-efficiency furnaces, boilers, and air conditioners, along with programmable thermostats and zoning systems, optimize energy use. Additionally, regular maintenance and timely upgrades of HVAC systems ensure their optimal performance.

Renewable Energy Integration

Incorporating renewable energy sources, such as solar, wind, or geothermal, can significantly reduce a building's reliance on fossil fuels. Solar panels, for instance, can be installed on rooftops or integrated into building facades to generate electricity. Geothermal systems, which utilize the stable underground temperatures for heating and cooling, offer another viable option. Combining these technologies with energy storage solutions, such as batteries, can further enhance a building's energy resilience and sustainability.

Lighting Efficiency

Lighting is another area where significant energy savings can be achieved. The transition from incandescent bulbs to energy-efficient LED lighting has revolutionized the industry. LEDs consume a fraction of the energy and have a much longer lifespan. Beyond the choice of bulbs, incorporating natural light through skylights, light tubes, and large windows can reduce the need for artificial lighting during the day. Additionally, automated lighting controls, such as occupancy sensors and daylight harvesting systems, ensure that lights are only used when necessary.

Water Efficiency

While often overlooked, water efficiency is an integral part of sustainable building design. Reducing water consumption not only conserves a precious resource but also reduces the energy required for water heating and pumping. Low-flow fixtures, rainwater harvesting systems, and greywater recycling are some of the strategies that can be employed to enhance water efficiency.

Smart Building Technologies

The advent of smart building technologies has opened new avenues for energy efficiency. Building management systems (BMS) and Internet of Things (IoT) devices enable real-time monitoring and control of energy use.

Smart thermostats, lighting systems, and appliances can adapt to occupancy patterns and environmental conditions, optimizing energy consumption. Moreover, predictive maintenance, enabled by data analytics, can identify potential issues before they lead to energy wastage.

Successful Implementation of Energy-Efficient Designs

Examining real-world examples can provide valuable insights into the practical application of energy-efficient building design principles. Let's explore a few notable case studies:

The Bullitt Center, Seattle, once dubbed the 'greenest commercial building in the world,' the Bullitt Center in Seattle is a showcase of sustainable design. The building features a rooftop solar array that generates all the electricity it needs, a rainwater harvesting system that meets its water requirements, and composting toilets that minimise water use. Advanced insulation and a highly efficient HVAC system further enhance its energy performance.

Eden, Manchester A landmark project in Manchester, the Eden, was completed in January 2024. Exceeding the UK Green Building Council's 2030-2035 operational energy targets, it is Britain's most sustainable office buildings with a projected annual energy consumption of 41kWh/m2. The construction followed Passivhaus principles, has a 60:40 solid-to-glazing ratio and is equipped with air-source heat pumps. Consequently, the Eden achieved a record 5.5 NABERS 'Design Reviewed' Target Rating. The use of natural light and energy-efficient lighting systems further contribute to its low energy consumption and is truly unique in the UK is it's green, living façade covered with plants.

Case Study 3: The Edge, Amsterdam The Edge in Amsterdam is often referred to as the smartest building in the world. Its energy-efficient design includes rooftop solar panels, rainwater harvesting, and a highly efficient HVAC system. The building's smart technologies, such as a connected lighting system and an app that personalises workspaces, optimize energy use based on occupancy and individual preferences. In The Edge, employees no longer have assigned desks. This allows them to work anywhere in the building in varying levels of introspection or sociability: there are work booths, focus rooms, concentration rooms, sitting desks, standing desks, and balcony desks, along with the many workstations within the sun-filled atrium itself.

Retrofitting Existing Buildings for Energy Efficiency

While designing new buildings with energy efficiency in mind is crucial, retrofitting existing structures also offers significant opportunities for energy savings. Retrofitting involves updating building systems and components to improve their energy performance.

- Energy Audits and Benchmarking - The first step in any retrofit project is to conduct a comprehensive energy audit. This involves assessing the building's current energy use, identifying inefficiencies, and benchmarking its performance against similar structures. Tools like the Energy Star Portfolio Manager can provide valuable data for this analysis.
- Building Envelope Improvements - Enhancing the building envelope is often the most cost-effective retrofit measure. This includes upgrading insulation, sealing air leaks, and installing energy-efficient windows and doors. These improvements can significantly reduce heating and cooling loads, leading to substantial energy savings.
- HVAC System Upgrades - Retrofitting HVAC systems is another critical step. Replacing outdated equipment with high-efficiency models, installing variable speed drives, and optimizing control systems can improve the overall performance of HVAC systems. Additionally, implementing demand-controlled ventilation, which adjusts airflow based on occupancy, can further enhance energy efficiency.
- Lighting Retrofits - Lighting retrofits offer quick and often highly cost-effective energy savings. Replacing outdated lighting fixtures with LED alternatives, installing occupancy sensors, and integrating daylighting controls can significantly reduce energy consumption.
- Renewable Energy Retrofits - Integrating renewable energy sources into existing buildings can also be highly beneficial. Solar panels, wind turbines, and geothermal systems can be retrofitted to existing structures, reducing their reliance on grid electricity and fossil fuels. Additionally, implementing energy storage solutions can enhance the building's energy resilience.

Financing and Incentives for Energy-Efficient Retrofits

One of the challenges of retrofitting existing buildings is the upfront cost. However, various financing options and incentives are available to support energy-efficient retrofits.

Government grants, utility rebates, and performance contracting are some of the mechanisms that can help offset the initial investment. Additionally, green building certifications, such as LEED and BREEAM, can enhance the market value of retrofitted buildings.

To conclude, energy-efficient building design and retrofitting are essential components of a sustainable future. By integrating advanced technologies, sustainable materials, and smart systems, buildings can significantly reduce their energy consumption and environmental impact.

Whether constructing new buildings or retrofitting existing ones, a comprehensive approach to energy efficiency can lead to substantial savings, improved occupant comfort, and a greener planet.

4.3 Harnessing the Power of the Sun: Solar Energy for Enhanced Efficiency

As the world grapples with the pressing need to mitigate climate change and reduce greenhouse gas emissions, the adoption of renewable energy sources has become a cornerstone of sustainable management. Among these sources, solar energy stands out as a powerful and versatile option, offering significant opportunities for enhancing efficiency and achieving long-term sustainability goals. In this section, we will look again at the myriad benefits of solar energy, explore the various technologies and applications available, and provide practical guidance on implementing solar solutions within your organization.

<u>Understanding Solar Energy</u>
Solar energy, derived from the sun's radiation, is an abundant and inexhaustible resource. It can be harnessed through various technologies, primarily photovoltaic (PV) panels and solar thermal systems. The former converts sunlight directly into electricity, while the latter captures and utilizes the sun's heat for various applications, such as water heating and industrial processes. The versatility of solar energy makes it an attractive option for organizations seeking to reduce their reliance on fossil fuels and enhance their energy efficiency.

The Benefits of Solar Energy
Solar energy offers a plethora of benefits that make it a compelling choice for businesses aiming to improve their energy efficiency. Some of the key advantages include:

1. Environmental Impact: Solar energy is a clean and renewable source of power, producing no greenhouse gas emissions during operation. By transitioning to solar energy, organizations can significantly reduce their carbon footprint and contribute to global efforts to combat climate change.
2. Cost Savings: While the initial investment in solar energy systems can be substantial, the long-term savings on energy bills are considerable. Solar panels have a lifespan of 25-30 years, during which time they can generate significant cost savings by reducing or even eliminating electricity bills.
3. Energy Independence: Solar energy enables organizations to generate their own power, reducing their dependence on external energy suppliers and shielding them from volatile energy prices. This energy independence can enhance operational stability and resilience.
4. Incentives and Rebates: Many governments and local authorities offer incentives, rebates, and tax credits to encourage the adoption of solar energy. These financial incentives can significantly offset the initial costs of installation and improve the return on investment.
5. Technological Advancements: Advances in solar technology have made it more efficient, affordable, and accessible than ever before. Innovations in PV panel efficiency, energy storage solutions, and solar integration with smart grids are continually enhancing the viability and attractiveness of solar energy.

Implementing Solar Solutions

The successful implementation of solar energy solutions requires careful planning, analysis, and execution. The following subsections provide a step-by-step guide to help organizations navigate this process and maximize the benefits of solar energy.

<u>Conducting a Solar Feasibility Study</u>
Before embarking on a solar energy project, it is essential to conduct a thorough feasibility study to assess the potential and suitability of solar energy for your organization. A comprehensive feasibility study should include:

- Site Assessment: Evaluate the physical characteristics of the site, including solar irradiance levels, shading, roof orientation, and available space for PV panels or solar thermal systems. Geographic location and climate conditions also play a crucial role in determining the potential solar energy yield.

- Energy Consumption Analysis: Analyze your organization's current and projected energy consumption patterns to determine the optimal size and capacity of the solar energy system. This analysis should consider peak demand periods, seasonal variations, and potential future growth.
- Financial Analysis: Perform a detailed financial analysis to estimate the costs, savings, and payback period of the solar energy project. Consider factors such as installation costs, maintenance expenses, energy savings, and available incentives or rebates.
- Regulatory and Permitting Requirements: Research and understand the regulatory and permitting requirements for installing solar energy systems in your area. This may include obtaining building permits, grid connection approvals, and compliance with local zoning laws and safety standards.

Choosing the Right Solar Technology
Selecting the appropriate solar technology is crucial to the success of your solar energy project. The two primary technologies to consider are photovoltaic (PV) panels and solar thermal systems:

- Photovoltaic Panels: PV panels are the most common and widely used solar technology. They convert sunlight directly into electricity using semiconductor materials. PV systems can be installed on rooftops, ground-mounted, or integrated into building facades. When choosing PV panels, consider factors such as efficiency, durability, warranty, and the reputation of the manufacturer.
- Solar Thermal Systems: Solar thermal systems capture and utilize the sun's heat for various applications, such as water heating, space heating, and industrial processes. These systems are particularly effective in regions with high direct sunlight and can significantly reduce reliance on conventional heating sources. When selecting solar thermal systems, consider factors such as system type (e.g., flat-plate collectors, evacuated tube collectors), efficiency, and integration with existing heating infrastructure.

Note that there are also PVT panels in certain markets that provide both the electricity and the hot water and these applications may be appropriate in some cases.

Designing and Installing the Solar Energy System
Once the feasibility study is complete and the appropriate technology is

selected, the next step is to design and install the solar energy system. Key considerations during this phase include:

1. System Design: Work with experienced solar energy professionals to design a system that meets your organization's energy needs and site conditions. The design should optimize panel placement, orientation, and tilt angle to maximize solar energy capture. Additionally, consider the integration of energy storage solutions, such as batteries, to store excess energy for use during periods of low sunlight.
2. Installation: Engage certified and reputable solar installers to ensure the system is installed correctly and safely. The installation process should adhere to industry standards and best practices, including proper mounting, wiring, and connection to the electrical grid or existing heating systems.
3. Commissioning and Testing: Once the system is installed, it must be commissioned and tested to ensure it operates as intended. This involves verifying the performance of the panels, inverters, and other components, as well as checking for compliance with safety and regulatory requirements.

Monitoring and Maintenance

Effective monitoring and maintenance are essential to ensure the long-term performance and reliability of the solar energy system. Key practices include:

- Monitoring: Implement a robust monitoring system to track the performance of the solar energy system in real-time. This can include monitoring software, sensors, and data analytics tools that provide insights into energy production, system efficiency, and potential issues.
- Regular Maintenance: Schedule regular maintenance to keep the system operating at peak efficiency. This may include cleaning the panels to remove dust and debris, inspecting and tightening electrical connections, and checking for any signs of wear or damage.
- Periodic Inspections: Conduct periodic inspections by qualified professionals to assess the overall condition of the system and address any maintenance needs. These inspections should include a thorough review of all components, such as panels, inverters, mounting structures, and wiring.

- Updating and Upgrading: Stay informed about advancements in solar technology and consider updating or upgrading components as needed to enhance system performance. This may include replacing aging panels with more efficient ones, integrating new energy storage solutions, or adopting advanced monitoring and control technologies.

Case Studies: Successful Solar Energy Implementations

To illustrate the potential of solar energy for enhancing efficiency, let's explore a few case studies of organizations that have successfully implemented solar solutions:

- Solar-Powered Manufacturing Facility A leading manufacturing company in the automotive industry embarked on a mission to reduce its carbon footprint and enhance energy efficiency. After conducting a comprehensive feasibility study, the company installed a large-scale PV system on the rooftops of its manufacturing facilities. The solar panels generated enough electricity to meet a significant portion of the facility's energy needs, resulting in substantial cost savings and a marked reduction in greenhouse gas emissions. The company also integrated an energy storage solution to ensure a stable power supply during peak demand periods.
- Solar Thermal System for Industrial Heating A food processing plant in a sunny region sought to reduce its reliance on natural gas for industrial heating processes. The plant installed a solar thermal system with evacuated tube collectors to capture and utilize the sun's heat for water heating and steam generation. This transition to solar thermal energy not only reduced the plant's energy costs but also significantly lowered its carbon emissions. The success of the project prompted the plant to expand its solar thermal system and explore additional renewable energy opportunities.

Overcoming Challenges and Maximizing Benefits

While solar energy offers numerous advantages, organizations may encounter challenges during the implementation process. Addressing these challenges proactively can help maximize the benefits of solar energy:

1. Initial Investment: The upfront cost of solar energy systems can be a barrier for some organizations. To overcome this, explore financing options such as power purchase agreements (PPAs), leasing arrangements, and available incentives or rebates. These options can help

spread the costs over time and improve the financial feasibility of the project.
2. Grid Integration: Integrating solar energy systems with the electrical grid can present technical and regulatory challenges. Work closely with utility companies and regulatory authorities to ensure a smooth grid connection and compliance with all requirements. Additionally, consider incorporating energy storage solutions to enhance grid stability and support a reliable power supply.
3. Space Limitations: Limited space for installing solar panels can constrain the scale of the project. Explore innovative solutions such as building-integrated photovoltaics (BIPV), which integrate solar panels into the building structure, or ground-mounted systems in available open spaces. Additionally, consider partnering with neighbouring businesses or community solar programs to share resources and maximize solar energy potential. Community projects may also be an option.
4. Maintenance and Longevity: Ensuring the long-term performance and reliability of solar energy systems requires ongoing maintenance and monitoring. Establish a comprehensive maintenance plan and allocate resources for regular inspections, cleaning, and component replacements. Leveraging advanced monitoring technologies can also help identify and address potential issues before they impact system performance.

Harnessing solar energy presents a transformative opportunity for organizations to enhance their energy efficiency, reduce emissions, and achieve long-term sustainability goals.

By understanding the benefits, conducting thorough feasibility studies, selecting the right technology, and implementing best practices for design, installation, and maintenance, organizations can unlock the full potential of solar energy.

As demonstrated by successful case studies, the transition to solar energy not only drives cost savings and environmental benefits but also positions organizations as leaders in the global movement towards a greener future. With the right approach and commitment, solar energy can become a cornerstone of your organization's sustainable management strategy.

4.4 Behavioural Changes and Employee Engagement

In the quest for enhanced efficiency, it's easy to overlook the immense impact of human behaviour. Yet, behavioural changes are often the most cost-effective and immediately actionable pathways to improvement.

Unlike technological upgrades, which can require substantial capital investment and time to implement, behavioural changes can be initiated almost immediately with the right strategies and tools. We will now explore the pivotal role that employee engagement plays in driving these changes and how managers can foster a culture of sustainability within their organizations.

Sustainability is as much a Problem of Marketing, as it is Technology - JH

Understanding the Psychology of Change

To effectively engage employees in energy efficiency initiatives, it's crucial to understand the psychology behind behavioural change. The adoption of new habits often follows a predictable pattern: Awareness, Interest, Trial, and Adoption.

Managers should aim to guide employees through each of these stages by providing the necessary information, creating interest through compelling narratives, and enabling easy trials of new behaviours.

Awareness: The First Step

Raising awareness is the foundational step in driving behavioural change. Employees must first recognize the importance of energy efficiency and how their actions contribute to the organization's overall sustainability goals. This can be achieved through various means such as workshops, informational meetings, and internal communications that highlight the current state of energy consumption and its environmental impact.

Creating Interest

Once awareness is established, the next step is to generate interest. This can be done by connecting energy efficiency to values *that employees care about*, such as environmental stewardship, cost savings, or corporate social responsibility. Storytelling can be a powerful tool here; sharing success stories from within the organization or from industry leaders can inspire employees and make the concept of energy efficiency more relatable and attainable.

Enabling Trial
For employees to adopt new behaviours, they need opportunities to experiment with them in a risk-free environment. Managers can facilitate this by setting up pilot projects or challenges that encourage employees to try out new energy-saving practices. Providing the necessary resources and support during this trial phase is crucial for building confidence and demonstrating the feasibility of the proposed changes and simply getting 'buy-in' from stakeholders.

Adoption: Making It Stick
The final stage is adoption, where new behaviours become ingrained in the daily routines of employees. This requires continuous reinforcement through positive feedback, recognition, and incentives. Monitoring and reporting on the progress of energy-saving initiatives can also help maintain momentum and demonstrate the tangible impact of these behavioural changes.

Strategies for Fostering Employee Engagement

To successfully drive behavioural changes, managers must create an environment that fosters employee engagement. Here are some actionable strategies to achieve this:

Leadership Begins At The Top
Leadership plays a critical role in setting the tone for organizational culture. When leaders actively participate in and advocate for energy efficiency initiatives, it sends a powerful message to employees about the importance of these efforts. Leaders should lead by example, demonstrating their commitment through their actions and decisions. This could include simple acts like turning off lights when leaving a room, using energy-efficient appliances, or participating in energy-saving challenges.

Communication and Education
Clear and consistent communication is essential for keeping employees informed and motivated. Regular updates on energy efficiency goals, progress, and achievements can help maintain interest and engagement. Educational initiatives such as workshops, training sessions, and informational campaigns can equip employees with the knowledge and skills they need to contribute effectively. Providing practical tips and guidelines for energy-saving behaviours can also make it easier for employees to take action.

Incentives and Recognition
Incentives and recognition can be powerful motivators for encouraging

desired behaviours. Managers can implement reward programs that recognize and celebrate employees who make significant contributions to energy efficiency. This could include financial incentives, public recognition, or other forms of appreciation. Creating a sense of competition, such as departmental challenges or individual achievements, can also spur employees to take proactive steps toward energy conservation.

Collaborative Initiatives and Employee Involvement
It is crucial to involve employees in the planning and implementation of energy efficiency initiatives to enhance their sense of ownership and commitment. Managers must actively seek input and feedback from employees at all levels and encourage them to share ideas and suggestions for improvement. Establishing collaborative initiatives, such as green teams or sustainability committees, is essential to providing a platform for employees to actively participate and contribute to the organization's energy-saving efforts.

Practical Examples of Behavioural Changes
To illustrate the practical application of these strategies, let's explore some examples of behavioural changes that can significantly impact energy efficiency:

Office Lighting
Encouraging employees to turn off lights when not in use, utilize natural light whenever possible, and adopt energy-efficient lighting solutions can reduce energy consumption significantly. Installing motion sensors or timers can further automate this process and ensure lights are only on when needed.

Equipment and Appliance Usage
Educating employees about the energy consumption of office equipment and appliances can lead to more mindful usage. Simple actions like turning off computers, printers, and other devices when not in use, using power strips to easily disconnect multiple devices, and opting for energy-efficient models can collectively result in substantial energy savings.

Heating and Cooling Practices
Optimizing heating and cooling practices can have a significant impact on energy efficiency. Encouraging employees to dress appropriately for the season, utilize natural ventilation, and adjust thermostats to energy-saving settings can reduce the demand for heating and cooling. Implementing programmable thermostats and zoning systems can further enhance control and efficiency.

Waste Reduction and Recycling

Promoting waste reduction and recycling practices can contribute to overall sustainability efforts. Encouraging employees to reduce paper usage, recycle materials, and properly dispose of waste can minimize the environmental impact of office operations. Providing easily accessible recycling bins and educating employees about proper recycling practices can facilitate participation.

Measuring and Sustaining Behavioural Changes

To ensure the long-term success of behavioural changes, it's essential to measure and sustain these efforts. Here are some key steps to achieve this:

Monitoring and Reporting

Regular monitoring and reporting on energy consumption and the impact of behavioural changes can provide valuable insights and help track progress. Utilizing energy management software or conducting periodic audits can identify areas of improvement and highlight successful initiatives. Sharing these findings with employees can reinforce the importance of their efforts and motivate continued engagement.

Continuous Improvement

Behavioural changes should be viewed as an ongoing process rather than a one-time effort. Managers should continually seek opportunities for improvement and innovation. This can involve conducting surveys or feedback sessions to gather input from employees, staying updated on industry best practices, and exploring new technologies or strategies that can further enhance energy efficiency.

Long-Term Commitment and Culture Building

Sustaining behavioural changes requires a long-term commitment to building a culture of sustainability within the organization. This involves integrating energy efficiency principles into the organization's values, policies, and practices. Managers should consistently communicate the importance of energy efficiency, celebrate successes, and reinforce desired behaviours. By embedding sustainability into the organizational culture, employees are more likely to embrace and sustain energy-saving practices over the long term.

Behavioural changes and employee engagement are powerful drivers of energy efficiency and sustainability within organizations. By understanding the psychology of change, fostering employee engagement, and implementing practical strategies, managers can create a culture of sustainability that leads to significant energy savings and environmental impact. The journey towards enhanced efficiency begins with small, actionable steps that, when collectively adopted, can make a substantial difference. By prioritizing behavioural changes and engaging employees at every level, organizations can pave the way for a greener, more sustainable future.

4.5 Quantifying the ROI of Sustainability Initiatives

As companies are increasingly recognizing the importance of integrating sustainable practices into their operations to ensure long-term success, so too has the pressure to sponsor initiatives that actually work for an increasingly critical audience. Executives and stakeholders alike often need to be convinced of the tangible benefits that sustainability initiatives can bring. This is where quantifying the return on investment (ROI) of these initiatives becomes essential. By demonstrating the financial benefits that sustainable practices can offer, managers can build a compelling case for their adoption.

This intricate and often iterative process of quantifying the ROI of sustainability initiatives is the subject of this section. We will explore various metrics, methodologies, and case studies to provide a comprehensive understanding of how to measure and communicate the financial advantages of going green.

Understanding ROI in the Context of Sustainability

Return on Investment (ROI) is a performance measure used to evaluate the efficiency or profitability of an investment. In the context of sustainability, ROI represents the financial returns derived from investments in sustainable practices. These returns can come in various forms, including cost savings, revenue generation, and enhanced brand reputation.

<u>Types of ROI Metrics</u>
1. Cost Savings: One of the most straightforward ways to quantify ROI is through cost savings. This can include reductions in energy consumption, water usage, and waste generation. For example, implementing energy-efficient lighting and HVAC systems can result in significant savings on utility bills.
2. Revenue Generation: Sustainable practices can also generate new revenue streams. For instance, companies that invest in renewable energy sources can sell excess energy back to the grid. Additionally, developing eco-friendly products can attract new customers and open up new markets.
3. Brand Value and Reputation: While more challenging to quantify, the

positive impact on brand value and reputation cannot be overlooked. Companies that are perceived as environmentally responsible can enjoy increased customer loyalty, attract top talent, and benefit from favourable media coverage.

Methodologies for Quantifying ROI

Life Cycle Cost Analysis (LCCA)
Life Cycle Cost Analysis (LCCA) is a comprehensive method for evaluating the total cost of ownership of a project or investment over its entire life cycle. This includes initial costs, operational costs, maintenance costs, and end-of-life disposal costs. By comparing the life cycle costs of sustainable options versus traditional options, managers can identify the long-term financial benefits of sustainable practices.

Total Cost of Ownership (TCO)
Total Cost of Ownership (TCO) is another valuable methodology for quantifying ROI. TCO takes into account all direct and indirect costs associated with an investment. For sustainability initiatives, this can include costs related to procurement, implementation, operation, and disposal. By calculating TCO, managers can gain a holistic view of the financial impact of sustainability investments.

Payback Period
The payback period is the amount of time it takes for an investment to generate enough savings to cover its initial cost. This metric is particularly useful for sustainability initiatives that involve significant upfront costs. For example, the payback period for installing solar panels can be calculated by dividing the initial installation cost by the annual energy savings.

A Couple Of Real-World Examples

Walmart's Energy Efficiency Program
Walmart, one of the world's largest retailers, has made significant investments in energy efficiency. By upgrading to LED lighting in its stores and distribution centers, Walmart has achieved substantial cost savings. The initial investment in LED lighting was offset by the reduction in energy consumption, resulting in a short payback period and ongoing savings.

Their Big-Box Efficiency Project evaluated the benefits of combining five different energy efficiency measures:

- Efficient, direct current-capable LED lighting.

- Smart motors for refrigeration and heating, ventilation and air conditioning.
- Precooling outside air using water and evaporation to reduce electricity needed for air conditioning.
- Smart water management to reduce waste.
- An Internet of Things building energy management systems platform to analyse data and identify energy savings opportunities.

Unilever's Sustainable Living Plan
Unilever's Sustainable Living Plan focuses on reducing the environmental impact of its products and operations. By implementing energy-efficient technologies and optimizing supply chains, Unilever has not only reduced its carbon footprint but also achieved significant cost savings. The company's commitment to sustainability has also enhanced its brand reputation, leading to increased customer loyalty and market share.

Communicating the Financial Benefits

To secure buy-in from executives and stakeholders, it is crucial to effectively communicate the financial benefits of sustainability initiatives. This involves presenting clear and concise data, backed by robust methodologies and real-world examples.

Key Points to Communicate
1. Cost Savings: Highlight the immediate and long-term cost savings that can be achieved through sustainable practices. Use concrete data and case studies to illustrate these savings.
2. Revenue Generation: Showcase potential new revenue streams that can be created through sustainability initiatives. Provide examples of companies that have successfully leveraged sustainability for revenue growth.
3. Brand Value: Emphasize the positive impact on brand value and reputation. Present data on customer preferences for environmentally responsible companies and the competitive advantage this can offer.

Tools and Resources
1. ROI Calculators: There are various online tools and calculators that can help quantify the ROI of sustainability initiatives, these are available on both government and private sites across the world and often tailored to fit the local economy to provide a quick view of potential savings and returns.
2. Consulting Services: Engaging with sustainability consultants can provide

valuable insights and expertise. Consultants can conduct detailed analyses and develop customized ROI models for specific initiatives.
3. Industry Reports: Leverage industry reports and research studies that provide data on the financial benefits of sustainability. These reports can serve as credible sources to support your case.

Overcoming Challenges

Quantifying the ROI of sustainability initiatives can be challenging due to the complexity of measuring intangible benefits and long-term impacts. However, by adopting a systematic approach and leveraging the right tools and methodologies, these challenges can be effectively addressed.

Addressing Intangible Benefits
While cost savings and revenue generation are relatively straightforward to quantify, intangible benefits such as brand value and employee engagement can be more challenging. To address this, consider using qualitative data and surveys to capture the impact of sustainability on these areas. For example, employee surveys can provide insights into how sustainability initiatives influence job satisfaction and retention.

Long-Term vs. Short-Term Focus
Executives and stakeholders often prioritize short-term financial gains over long-term benefits. To overcome this challenge, it is essential to present a balanced view that highlights both immediate and future returns. Use scenarios and projections to illustrate the cumulative benefits of sustainability initiatives over time.

Quantifying the ROI of sustainability initiatives is a critical step in building a compelling case for their adoption. By understanding the various metrics and methodologies, and effectively communicating the financial benefits, managers can secure the support needed to drive sustainable practices within their organizations. As the corporate world continues to evolve, those who can demonstrate the tangible value of sustainability will be well-positioned to lead their organizations towards a greener, more prosperous future.

Conclusion: Enhancing Efficiency for a Sustainable Future

In Chapter 4, we explored various strategies that can significantly enhance efficiency and sustainability within your organization.

By identifying and prioritizing improvement areas, you can focus your efforts on the most impactful initiatives.

Adopting energy-efficient building designs and retrofitting existing structures can lead to substantial energy savings and reduced operational costs.

Leveraging renewable energy sources further supports your sustainability goals, offering long-term environmental and economic benefits.

Behavioural changes and employee engagement are crucial for fostering a culture of sustainability. Educating and involving your team can drive meaningful, lasting change.

Finally, quantifying the ROI of sustainability initiatives helps in demonstrating their value and securing ongoing support from stakeholders.

Key takeaways include:

- the importance of a systematic approach to identifying improvement opportunities
- the benefits of energy-efficient design and renewable energy
- the role of employee engagement in driving sustainability
- the necessity of measuring the financial impact of your initiatives.

By implementing these strategies, you can not only enhance efficiency but also contribute to a greener and more sustainable future for your organization.

5 SUSTAINABLE GREEN PRACTICES: LONG-TERM STRATEGIES

Source: Pexels - Photo by Maria Orlova:

As we approach the second half of the 2020s, the concept of sustainability and the part a circular economy will play in business operations has evolved from being a mere trend to an essential business imperative.

The initial strides toward sustainable practices, such as implementing energy-efficient systems or reducing emissions, are undoubtedly significant. However, the true challenge lies in sustaining these practices over the long term. Chapter 5 of 'Green from Green II - Businesses & Utilities' considers several critical strategies necessary for maintaining and enhancing your organization's green initiatives well into the future.

Creating a culture of sustainability within an organization is to long-term success as the keystone was to an old stone bridge. This goes beyond policy implementation; it's about fostering an environment where every employee, from the top executives to the entry-level staff, is committed to sustainable practices. We will explore how to instill this culture through effective communication, leadership commitment, and employee engagement. By embedding sustainability into your corporate DNA, you ensure that green practices are not just a mandate but a shared value.

Continuous monitoring and optimization are vital for sustaining green practices. In this chapter, we will examine the tools and technologies that enable ongoing assessment and improvement of energy consumption and emissions. By leveraging advanced analytics and real-time data, managers can make informed decisions, identify inefficiencies, and quickly adapt to changing circumstances. This proactive approach ensures that sustainable practices are not only maintained but also continually refined for better performance and cost savings.

Training and development play a crucial role in equipping your workforce with the necessary competencies to support sustainable initiatives. We will discuss various training programs, certifications, and workshops that can help build green skills within your organization. Investing in the development of your team not only enhances their capabilities but also demonstrates your commitment to sustainability, fostering a more engaged and motivated workforce.

Building partnerships with green organizations can amplify your sustainability efforts. These collaborations can provide access to new technologies, innovative solutions, and valuable insights that can drive your green agenda forward. We will explore how to identify and establish mutually beneficial partnerships with industry leaders, non-profits, and governmental bodies, creating a network of support that can help sustain and expand your green initiatives.

Looking ahead, we will consider future trends in sustainable management that are set to shape the coming decade. From advancements in renewable energy and smart grid technologies to evolving regulatory landscapes and consumer expectations, staying ahead of these trends is crucial. We will also touch on ESG (Environmental, Social, and Governance) management and ESG financial assets and trading as powerful tools for improving your organization's bottom line while enhancing its sustainability profile.

By the end of this chapter, you will be equipped with a robust framework for sustaining green practices in your organization. The strategies discussed will not only help you maintain momentum but also drive continuous improvement, ensuring that your organization remains at the forefront of sustainable management in the 2020s and beyond. Whether you are just beginning your sustainability journey or looking to enhance your existing efforts, the insights and practical advice in this chapter will provide the guidance you need to achieve long-term success.

5.1 Creating a Culture of Sustainability

In the dynamic landscape of the 2020s, creating a culture of sustainability within an organization is not just a noble endeavor; it is a business imperative. A well-ingrained culture of sustainability can drive innovation, enhance employee morale, and improve the bottom line.

This section re-examines many of the key strategies and principles essential for embedding sustainability into the core of your organization.

The Importance of Leadership Commitment

Leadership plays a pivotal role in cultivating a culture of sustainability. It begins with the top executives and filters down through every layer of the organization. Leaders must not only endorse sustainability initiatives but also actively participate and model sustainable behaviors.

This commitment can be demonstrated through clear communication, setting achievable goals, and providing the necessary resources for sustainability projects. When employees see leaders who are genuinely engaged in sustainability efforts, it fosters a sense of shared purpose and motivation.

<u>Setting Clear and Achievable Goals</u>

To build a sustainable culture, organizations must establish clear, measurable goals. These goals should align with the broader strategic objectives of the company and be realistic yet ambitious. Utilizing frameworks such as the SMART criteria—Specific, Measurable, Achievable, Relevant, and Time-bound—can help in setting effective sustainability goals. Regularly reviewing and adjusting these goals based on performance and evolving circumstances ensures that the sustainability culture remains dynamic and forward-thinking.

<u>Employee Engagement and Education</u>

Engaging employees in sustainability efforts is crucial for the success of any initiative. This begins with education and training programs designed to raise awareness about sustainability issues and solutions. Workshops, seminars, and online courses can be used to equip employees with the knowledge and skills necessary to contribute to sustainability goals. Additionally, creating platforms for employees to share their ideas and innovations can foster a sense of ownership and involvement.

Integrating Sustainability into Daily Operations
For sustainability to become part of the organizational culture, it must be integrated into daily operations. This involves revisiting and redesigning processes to minimize waste, conserve energy, and reduce emissions. For example, adopting energy-efficient technologies, implementing recycling programs, and encouraging telecommuting can significantly reduce the environmental footprint of an organization. Moreover, sustainability should be considered in decision-making processes across all levels of the organization.

Recognizing and Rewarding Sustainable Practices
Recognition and rewards are powerful tools for reinforcing sustainable behaviors. Organizations can establish reward systems that acknowledge individual and team contributions to sustainability goals. This can include monetary incentives, public recognition, and opportunities for professional development. By celebrating successes and highlighting best practices, organizations can motivate employees to continue their efforts towards sustainability.

Communicating Sustainability Efforts
Transparent and effective communication is essential for sustaining a culture of sustainability. This involves regularly updating all stakeholders—employees, customers, investors, and the community—about the organization's sustainability initiatives and progress. Utilizing various communication channels such as newsletters, social media, and annual sustainability reports can help in maintaining transparency and building trust. Clear communication also ensures that everyone is aligned with the sustainability vision and goals.

Leveraging ESG Management and Financial Assets
Environmental, Social, and Governance (ESG) management has emerged as a critical component of modern business strategy. By integrating ESG principles into business operations, organizations can enhance their sustainability performance and attract socially responsible investors.

ESG financial assets and trading can provide a significant boost to the bottom line or be an effective source of funding on larger and community projects. This involves investing in green bonds, sustainable funds, and other financial instruments that support environmental and social goals. Additionally, organizations can participate in carbon trading markets to offset their emissions and generate revenue from surplus carbon credits.

Creating a Sustainable Supply Chain
A sustainable culture extends beyond the organization and into its supply chain. Organizations must work closely with suppliers to ensure that sustainable practices are upheld throughout the supply chain. This includes selecting suppliers who adhere to environmental standards, conducting regular audits, and collaborating on sustainability initiatives. By fostering strong relationships with sustainable suppliers, organizations can mitigate risks and enhance their overall sustainability performance.

The Role of Technology in Sustainability
Technology plays a crucial role in advancing sustainability efforts. Innovations such as the Internet of Things (IoT), artificial intelligence (AI), and blockchain can be leveraged to enhance energy efficiency, reduce waste, and improve transparency. For instance, IoT devices can monitor and optimize energy usage in real-time, while AI algorithms can predict and manage resource consumption. Blockchain technology will in time help to ensure the integrity and traceability of sustainability data, thereby building trust among stakeholders.

Overcoming Challenges in Creating a Sustainable Culture
Creating a culture of sustainability is not without its challenges. Resistance to change, limited resources, the politicization of the environment and lack of awareness or apathy are all common obstacles.

To overcome these challenges, organizations must adopt a strategic and inclusive approach. This involves engaging all stakeholders, providing continuous education and support, and demonstrating the tangible benefits of sustainability. By addressing these challenges head-on, organizations can pave the way for a resilient and sustainable future.

Building a culture of sustainability requires a holistic and ongoing effort. It demands leadership commitment, clear goals, employee engagement, integration into daily operations, recognition of sustainable practices, effective communication, leveraging ESG management, sustainable supply chains, and the strategic use of technology.

The journey towards sustainability is continuous, but with the right strategies and commitment, it is a journey well worth undertaking.

5.2 Continuous Monitoring and Optimization

Wish that it were simple but the journey to sustainability does not end with the implementation of green practices. Continuous monitoring and optimization are critical components that ensure the longevity and effectiveness of these practices.

This section investigates the importance of ongoing scrutiny and fine-tuning, exploring the methodologies, tools, and case studies that demonstrate successful continuous monitoring and optimization in the realm of sustainable management.

The Necessity of Continuous Monitoring

Continuous monitoring is the backbone of any sustainable management strategy. It allows organizations to track their performance in real time, identify inefficiencies, and make informed decisions about where to allocate resources.

Continuous monitoring involves the regular collection and analysis of data related to energy consumption, emissions, and other environmental metrics. By maintaining a constant eye on these metrics, companies can ensure that they are adhering to their sustainability goals and making progress toward their targets.

Benefits of Continuous Monitoring
1. Real-Time Data: Access to real-time data allows for immediate action to be taken when deviations from the plan occur. This can prevent small issues from becoming significant problems.
2. Improved Decision-Making: With accurate and up-to-date information, managers can make better-informed decisions that contribute to the overall efficiency and sustainability of the organization.
3. Cost Savings: By identifying areas of waste and inefficiency, continuous monitoring can lead to significant cost savings. This is particularly important in the context of energy consumption and emissions reduction.
4. Regulatory Compliance: Governments and regulatory bodies are increasingly imposing stringent environmental standards. Continuous monitoring ensures that organizations remain compliant with these regulations, avoiding potential fines and sanctions.

Tools and Technologies for Continuous Monitoring
The advent of advanced technologies has revolutionized the way

organizations monitor and optimize their sustainability efforts. Several tools and technologies facilitate continuous monitoring, including:

1. Smart Meters: Smart meters provide real-time data on energy consumption, allowing organizations to identify patterns and trends that can inform optimization strategies.
2. IoT Sensors: Internet of Things (IoT) sensors can be deployed throughout a facility to monitor various environmental parameters, such as temperature, humidity, and air quality. These sensors provide granular data that can be used to fine-tune operations.
3. Energy Management Systems (EMS): EMS integrate data from various sources to provide a comprehensive view of an organization's energy usage. These systems often include analytics capabilities that can identify inefficiencies and suggest optimization strategies.
4. Cloud Computing Services: Cloud-based platforms enable organizations to store and analyze vast amounts of data without the need for significant on-premises infrastructure. This facilitates more efficient data processing and analysis.
5. Artificial Intelligence (AI) and Machine Learning (ML): AI and ML algorithms can analyze historical data to identify patterns and predict future trends. This predictive capability can help organizations anticipate and mitigate potential issues before they arise.

Case Study: Continuous Monitoring in Practice

To illustrate the impact of continuous monitoring, consider the case of a multinational manufacturing company that implemented an advanced energy management system across its facilities. By deploying smart meters and IoT sensors, the company was able to collect real-time data on energy consumption, machine performance, and environmental conditions.

Using this data, the company identified several areas of inefficiency, such as machines that were consuming excess energy during idle periods and HVAC systems that were not optimally calibrated. By addressing these issues, the company was able to reduce its energy consumption by 15% within the first year, resulting in significant cost savings and a reduction in its carbon footprint.

The Role of Optimization in Sustainable Management
While continuous monitoring provides the data needed to identify

inefficiencies, optimization is the process of making the necessary adjustments to improve performance. Optimization involves fine-tuning processes, equipment, and systems to achieve the best possible outcomes in terms of energy efficiency, emissions reduction, and overall sustainability.

Key Optimization Strategies
- Process Optimization: This involves analyzing and refining operational processes to minimize waste and maximize efficiency. Techniques such as Lean Manufacturing and Six Sigma can be employed to achieve process optimization.
- Equipment Optimization: Ensuring that equipment is operating at peak efficiency is crucial for reducing energy consumption. This may involve regular maintenance, upgrading to more energy-efficient models, or retrofitting existing equipment with advanced controls.
- System Optimization: This encompasses the optimization of entire systems, such as HVAC, lighting, and water management systems. By integrating these systems and using smart controls, organizations can achieve significant energy savings.
- Behavioral Optimization: Engaging employees and fostering a culture of sustainability can lead to behavioral changes that contribute to optimization. This may include training programs, incentives, and awareness campaigns.

Implementing Optimization: A Step-by-Step Approach
To effectively implement optimization the following steps could be considered:

1. Data Collection and Analysis: The first step is to collect and analyze data related to energy consumption, emissions, and other environmental metrics. This data will serve as the foundation for identifying areas of inefficiency and potential improvements.
2. Goal Setting: Based on the data analysis, organizations should set clear and achievable goals for optimization. These goals should be aligned with the overall sustainability objectives of the organization.
3. Action Planning: Develop a detailed action plan that outlines the specific optimization strategies to be implemented, along with timelines, responsibilities, and resource requirements.
4. Implementation: Execute the action plan, making the necessary adjustments to processes, equipment, and systems. This may involve

deploying new technologies, conducting training programs, or making operational changes.
5. Monitoring and Evaluation: Continuously monitor the performance of the implemented strategies to ensure that they are achieving the desired outcomes. Regularly evaluate the results and make further adjustments as needed.

Leveraging ESG Management for Continuous Improvement

Environmental, Social, and Governance (ESG) management has become an integral part of sustainable business practices. ESG management involves the integration of environmental, social, and governance factors into an organization's strategy and operations. By incorporating ESG principles, organizations can enhance their sustainability efforts and improve their long-term performance.

ESG Financial Assets and Trading

One of the ways organizations can leverage ESG management for continuous improvement is through the use of ESG financial assets and trading. ESG financial assets, such as green bonds and sustainability-linked loans, provide organizations with access to capital that is specifically earmarked for sustainable projects. These financial instruments often come with favourable terms and conditions, making them an attractive option for funding sustainability initiatives.

In addition, ESG trading involves the buying and selling of financial assets that meet specific ESG criteria. This can include stocks, bonds, and other securities that are issued by companies with strong ESG performance. By investing in ESG assets, organizations can not only support their sustainability goals but also potentially achieve higher financial returns.

Benefits of ESG Management
1. Enhanced Reputation: Organizations that prioritize ESG management are often viewed more favorably by stakeholders, including customers, investors, and regulators. This can lead to increased trust and loyalty.
2. Risk Mitigation: By addressing environmental, social, and governance risks, organizations can reduce their exposure to potential liabilities and disruptions.
3. Access to Capital: ESG financial assets and trading provide organizations with access to capital that can be used to fund sustainable projects and initiatives.

4. Improved Financial Performance: Studies have shown that companies with strong ESG performance often achieve better financial results, including higher profitability and lower volatility.

Continuous monitoring and optimization are essential components of a sustainable management strategy. By leveraging advanced tools and technologies, organizations can track their performance in real time, identify inefficiencies, and implement optimization strategies that enhance their sustainability efforts.

In addition, integrating ESG management can provide organizations with access to capital, enhance their reputation, and improve their long-term financial performance. By committing to continuous improvement, organizations can ensure the longevity and effectiveness of their green practices, ultimately leading to a more sustainable and prosperous future.

5.3 Training and Development for Green Competencies

In the dynamic landscape of modern business, the integration of sustainability into corporate practices is not just a trend but a necessity. As such, the role of training and development in fostering green competencies cannot be overstated. This section aims to provide a more in-depth guide on how organizations can cultivate a workforce that is proficient in sustainable practices, ensuring long-term success and resilience in an increasingly eco-conscious market.

Understanding Green Competencies

At the heart of any successful sustainability initiative lies a well-trained workforce equipped with the necessary green competencies. These competencies encompass a range of skills, knowledge, and attitudes that enable employees to contribute effectively to sustainability goals.

Green competencies are not limited to technical skills but also include strategic thinking, problem-solving, and an understanding of environmental impacts. Core Green Competencies

- Environmental Awareness: Understanding the impact of business activities on the environment and recognizing the importance of sustainability.
- Sustainable Practices: Knowledge of sustainable practices and how to implement them within the organization.
- Energy Management: Skills related to energy auditing, analysis, and the implementation of energy-saving measures.
- Waste Management: Competence in reducing waste, promoting recycling, and managing resources efficiently.

- Regulatory Compliance: Awareness of environmental regulations and the ability to ensure compliance.
- Strategic Thinking: The ability to integrate sustainability into business strategy and decision-making processes.
- Innovation and Problem-Solving: Skills to develop innovative solutions to sustainability challenges.

Designing Effective Training Programs
To build green competencies, organizations must invest in well-structured training programs. These programs should be tailored to the specific needs of the organization and its employees, ensuring that all relevant aspects of sustainability are covered.

- Needs Assessment The first step in designing an effective training program is conducting a thorough needs assessment. This involves identifying the specific green competencies required by the organization and assessing the current skill levels of employees. The needs assessment should take into account the organization's sustainability goals, regulatory requirements, and industry standards.
- Curriculum Development Based on the needs assessment, a comprehensive training curriculum can be developed. The curriculum should cover all core green competencies and include both theoretical and practical components. It is essential to incorporate real-world examples, case studies, and hands-on activities to reinforce learning.

Training Delivery Methods
The delivery of training programs can vary depending on the organization's resources and the preferences of employees. Some effective training delivery methods include:

- Workshops and Seminars: Interactive sessions that provide opportunities for discussion and collaboration.
- Online Courses: Flexible learning options that allow employees to complete training at their own pace.
- On-the-Job Training: Practical, hands-on training conducted in the workplace.
- Mentorship Programs: Pairing employees with experienced mentors to provide guidance and support.
- Certifications and Accreditation: Encouraging employees to pursue

certifications, such as those offered by the AEE Certified Energy Management curriculum.

Measuring Training Effectiveness
To ensure that training programs are effective in building green competencies, it is crucial to measure their impact. This can be achieved through various evaluation methods:

- Pre- and Post-Training Assessments Conducting assessments before and after training sessions can help gauge the improvement in employees' knowledge and skills. These assessments can include quizzes, practical tests, and self-evaluations.
- Feedback and Surveys Gathering feedback from participants through surveys and interviews can provide valuable insights into the effectiveness of the training program. This feedback can be used to make necessary adjustments and improvements.
- Performance Metrics - Monitoring key performance metrics related to sustainability goals can help determine the impact of training programs. Metrics such as energy consumption, waste reduction, and compliance with regulations can provide tangible evidence of the effectiveness of training.
- Continuous Improvement - Training and development should be an ongoing process. Regularly updating training programs to reflect the latest trends, technologies, and regulations is essential for maintaining green competencies. Continuous improvement ensures that employees remain knowledgeable and skilled in sustainable practices.

Leveraging ESG Management for Training and Development
Environmental, Social, and Governance (ESG) management plays a critical role in the development of green competencies. Integrating ESG principles into training programs can enhance the overall effectiveness and impact of sustainability initiatives.

- ESG Frameworks - ESG frameworks provide a structured approach to managing and reporting on sustainability performance. By aligning training programs with recognized ESG frameworks, organizations can ensure that their sustainability efforts are comprehensive and transparent.
- ESG Financial Assets and Trading - Understanding the financial aspects of ESG is crucial for managers and employees involved in sustainability

initiatives. Training programs should include modules on ESG financial assets, such as green bonds and sustainable investments, and their role in improving the bottom line.
- ESG Reporting and Compliance - Training employees on ESG reporting standards and compliance requirements is essential for maintaining transparency and accountability. This includes understanding the various reporting frameworks, such as the Global Reporting Initiative (GRI) and the Sustainability Accounting Standards Board (SASB).

Case Studies and Best Practices Learning from successful case studies and best practices can provide valuable insights and inspiration for developing green competencies. This section highlights a few exemplary organizations that have effectively integrated training and development into their sustainability strategies. Case Study 1: XYZ Corporation XYZ Corporation, a leading manufacturer, has implemented a comprehensive training program focused on energy management and waste reduction. By partnering with the AEE Certified Energy Management curriculum, XYZ has equipped its employees with the skills needed to conduct energy audits and implement energy-saving measures. As a result, the company has achieved significant reductions in energy consumption and waste generation, leading to substantial cost savings and improved environmental performance. Case Study 2: ABC Tech ABC Tech, a global technology company, has integrated ESG principles into its training and development programs. The company offers online courses and workshops on ESG financial assets, sustainable investments, and regulatory compliance. By educating its workforce on the financial and regulatory aspects of sustainability, ABC Tech has enhanced its ability to attract socially responsible investors and maintain compliance with global standards.

Best Practices –

Continuous Learning and Innovation - Leading organizations recognize the importance of continuous learning and innovation in building green competencies. They invest in ongoing training programs, encourage employees to pursue certifications, and foster a culture of innovation. By staying ahead of the curve, these organizations can adapt to evolving sustainability challenges and seize new opportunities.

Training and development for green competencies are essential components of a successful sustainability strategy. By equipping employees with the necessary skills and knowledge, organizations can drive meaningful change and achieve long-term sustainability goals. Through a combination of needs assessment, curriculum development, effective training delivery, and continuous improvement, organizations can build a workforce that is capable of navigating the complexities of the modern business environment while contributing to a greener future. Leveraging ESG management principles further enhances the impact of training programs, ensuring that sustainability efforts are comprehensive, transparent, and aligned with global standards. As we move forward into the 2020s, the importance of training and development in fostering green competencies will only continue to grow, making it a vital investment for any organization committed to sustainability.

5.4 Building Robust Partnerships with Green Organizations

In the quest for sustainability, one of the most powerful strategies is to forge strong sector and inter-sector partnerships with established green organizations. These alliances can create a synergistic effect, amplifying the impact of your green initiatives and ensuring long-term commitment to sustainable practices. Green organizations, with their wealth of knowledge, resources, and networks, can provide critical support and guidance to help you navigate the complexities of sustainable management.

The Importance of Green Partnerships

Enhancing Credibility and Trust

Aligning your organization with reputable green entities enhances your credibility and trust. Customers, stakeholders, and even employees are more likely to support and engage with a company that visibly commits to environmental stewardship. This trust is not just a feel-good factor; it translates into tangible business networking benefits, including enhanced customer loyalty, improved prospecting for increased sales, and a more engaged workforce.

Access to Expertise and Resources

Green organizations often have decades of experience and a deep understanding of the best sustainability practices. Partnering with these entities allows you to tap into their expertise, access cutting-edge research, and leverage their established resources. This can significantly accelerate your sustainability initiatives, helping you avoid common pitfalls and implement effective strategies more efficiently.

Shared Goals and Collaborative Projects
When you partner with green organizations, you align with entities that share your sustainability goals. This alignment opens opportunities for collaborative projects that can drive significant environmental impact. Whether it's joint industry research and development projects, shared sustainability campaigns, or co-hosted events, these collaborations can amplify your efforts and extend your reach.

Identifying the Right Green Partners
Research and Due Diligence
The first step in building robust partnerships is identifying the right organizations to partner with. This requires thorough research and due diligence. Look for organizations that align with your sustainability goals and values. Evaluate their track record, the impact of their initiatives, and their reputation in the industry.

Assessing Compatibility
Compatibility is crucial in any partnership. Assess the potential partner's culture, mission, and approach to sustainability. Ensure that there is a strong alignment with your organization's values and goals. This alignment will facilitate smoother collaboration and increase the likelihood of a successful partnership.

Establishing Clear, Mutually Agreed Objectives
Before formalizing any partnership, establish clear objectives and expectations. Define what you hope to achieve through the partnership and how success will be measured. Clear objectives will provide a roadmap for the partnership and ensure that both parties are working towards the same goals.

Case Studies: Successful Green Partnerships
Case Study 1: Unilever and WWF

Unilever, a global leader in consumer goods, has a long-standing partnership with the World Wildlife Fund (WWF). This collaboration focuses on improving the sustainability of Unilever's supply chain and reducing its environmental footprint. In Malaysia for example, WWF's Sabah Landscapes program combines conservation and sustainable development by integrating the protection of forests, wildlife and rivers into the production of RSPO-certified palm oil.

Through joint initiatives, Unilever and WWF have worked on projects ranging from sustainable sourcing of raw materials to reducing greenhouse gas emissions. This partnership has not only enhanced Unilever's sustainability credentials but also driven significant environmental impact.

Case Study 2: IKEA and The Nature Conservancy

IKEA, the world's largest furniture retailer, has partnered with The Nature Conservancy, recognizing "that the world is experiencing a biodiversity crisis. Dramatic loss of species, ecosystems and genetic diversity is human-induced and represents, together with climate change, one of the greatest challenges of our time." IKEA's wood-sourcing practices are sustainable and do not contribute to deforestation. Through joint projects, IKEA and The Nature Conservancy have developed innovative solutions to promote sustainable forestry and protect critical forest ecosystems.

Strategies for Building Effective Green Partnerships

Establishing Strong Communication Channels
Effective communication is the cornerstone of any successful partnership. Establish strong communication channels from the outset. Regular meetings, progress reports, and open lines of communication will ensure that both parties are aligned, and any issues are promptly addressed.

Building Trust and Mutual Respect
Trust and mutual respect are fundamental to a successful partnership. Be transparent about your goals, challenges, and expectations. Show genuine respect for your partner's expertise and contributions. Building a strong foundation of trust and respect will create a positive and collaborative partnership environment.

Leveraging Each Partner's Strengths
Each partner brings unique strengths and capabilities to the table. Leverage these strengths to maximize the impact of your partnership. Identify areas where your partner excels and can provide valuable support. Similarly, offer your strengths and resources to support your partner's initiatives.

ESG Management: Integrating Environmental, Social, and Governance Criteria

Environmental, Social, and Governance (ESG) criteria are increasingly becoming a critical component of sustainable business practices. ESG management involves integrating these criteria into your business strategy and operations. This holistic approach not only enhances your sustainability credentials but also improves your bottom line.

Environmental Criteria
Environmental criteria focus on a company's impact on the environment. This includes energy consumption, waste management, emissions reduction, and resource conservation. By integrating environmental criteria into your business practices, you can reduce your environmental footprint and contribute to global sustainability efforts.

Social Criteria
Social criteria consider a company's impact on society. This includes labor practices, community engagement, diversity and inclusion, and human rights. By prioritizing social criteria, you can create a positive social impact and build stronger relationships with your employees, customers, and communities.

Governance Criteria
Governance criteria evaluate a company's leadership, ethics, and transparency. This includes corporate governance structures, executive compensation, and stakeholder engagement. Strong governance practices ensure that your sustainability efforts are ethical, transparent, and accountable.

ESG Financial Assets and Trading
ESG investing, also known as sustainable investing, is gaining momentum in the financial markets. Investors are increasingly seeking opportunities to invest in companies that demonstrate strong ESG performance. This shift is driven by a growing recognition that sustainable companies are better positioned for long-term success.

Benefits of ESG Investing
ESG investing offers several benefits for businesses and investors. For businesses, strong ESG performance can attract investment, enhance reputation, and reduce risks. For investors, ESG investments offer the potential for strong financial returns and positive social and environmental impact.

ESG Financial Assets
ESG financial assets include stocks, bonds, and other investment vehicles that meet specific ESG criteria. These assets are evaluated based on their environmental, social, and governance performance. Investing in ESG financial assets allows companies to align their financial goals with their sustainability goals.

ESG Trading Platforms
Several trading platforms now offer ESG-specific investment options. These platforms provide tools and resources to help investors identify and invest in companies with strong ESG performance. By leveraging these platforms, businesses can attract ESG-focused investors and enhance their sustainability credentials.

Building robust partnerships with green organizations is a powerful strategy for sustaining green practices and achieving long-term sustainability goals. These partnerships provide access to expertise, resources, and networks that can amplify your sustainability efforts. By integrating ESG criteria into your business practices and leveraging ESG financial assets, you can enhance your sustainability credentials and improve your bottom line. Embrace the power of green partnerships and position your organization for sustainable success in the 2020s and beyond.

5.5 Future Trends in Sustainable Management

In the rapidly evolving landscape of sustainable management, future trends are poised to redefine how organizations approach their environmental responsibilities. The integration of Environmental, Social, and Governance (ESG) management and the growing significance of ESG financial assets and trading are becoming pivotal in enhancing the bottom line for businesses and utilities alike.

This section gives an overview of these emerging trends, providing a comprehensive understanding of their implications and how they can be leveraged for sustained green practices.

The Rise of ESG Management
ESG management has emerged as a critical framework for evaluating a company's commitment to sustainability, social responsibility, and ethical governance.

This is a holistic approach that goes beyond traditional financial metrics, encompassing a broad range of factors that reflect a company's impact on the environment, society, and its governance structures. The rise of the ESG management approach signifies a shift towards a more comprehensive evaluation of corporate performance, where sustainability is not just a peripheral concern but a core component of business strategy.

Environmental Stewardship
At the heart of ESG management is environmental stewardship. Companies are increasingly being held accountable for their environmental footprint, from carbon emissions to resource consumption. This accountability is driving innovation in sustainable practices, as businesses seek to not only comply with regulatory requirements but also to exceed them. Future trends in environmental stewardship include the adoption of advanced technologies for monitoring and reducing emissions, the integration of renewable energy sources, and the implementation of circular economy principles to minimize waste.

Social Responsibility
Social responsibility within the ESG framework focuses on a company's relationships with its employees, customers, and the broader community. This includes issues such as labor practices, diversity and inclusion, community engagement, and human rights. As stakeholders demand greater transparency and accountability, companies are adopting more robust social responsibility initiatives. These initiatives not only enhance a company's reputation but also contribute to a more sustainable and equitable society.

Governance
Governance in the context of ESG refers to the systems and processes that ensure a company operates ethically and transparently. This includes board diversity, executive compensation, risk management, and shareholder rights. Strong governance practices are essential for building trust with stakeholders and ensuring long-term sustainability. Future trends in governance include increased scrutiny of corporate leadership, greater emphasis on ethical decision-making, and the adoption of best practices for risk management.

The Financial Implications of ESG
The integration of ESG factors into financial decision-making is reshaping the investment landscape. Investors are increasingly recognizing that companies with strong ESG performance are better positioned to manage risks and capitalize on opportunities. This recognition is driving the growth of ESG financial assets and trading, as investors seek to align their portfolios with their values and sustainability goals.

ESG Financial Assets
ESG financial assets include a wide range of investment products that incorporate ESG criteria into their selection and management processes.

These assets can take various forms, including stocks, bonds, mutual funds, and exchange-traded funds (ETFs). ESG financial assets are designed to provide investors with exposure to companies that demonstrate strong environmental, social, and governance performance. The demand for these assets is growing rapidly, as investors increasingly prioritize sustainability in their investment decisions.

ESG Asset Trading
ESG asset trading involves the buying and selling of financial assets based on ESG criteria. This trend is gaining momentum as investors seek to capitalize on the financial benefits of sustainable investing. ESG trading strategies can include positive screening, where investors select companies based on their strong ESG performance, and negative screening, where companies with poor ESG performance are excluded from investment portfolios. Additionally, impact investing strategies focus on generating measurable social and environmental impacts alongside financial returns.

The Role of Technology in ESG Management
Technology is playing a crucial role in advancing ESG management and sustainable practices. Innovations in data analytics, artificial intelligence, and blockchain are transforming how companies monitor and report their ESG performance. These technologies enable more accurate and transparent reporting, enhance risk management, and support the development of innovative solutions to sustainability challenges.

Data Analytics and AI
Data analytics and artificial intelligence (AI) are revolutionizing ESG management by providing deeper insights into a company's environmental and social impacts. Advanced analytics tools can process vast amounts of data to identify trends, assess risks, and measure the effectiveness of sustainability initiatives. AI-powered platforms can help companies predict future ESG performance, optimize resource use, and develop targeted strategies for improvement.

Blockchain for Transparency
Blockchain technology offers unparalleled transparency and security in ESG reporting. By creating immutable records of transactions and data, blockchain can enhance the credibility of ESG reports and reduce the risk of greenwashing. Companies can use the blockchain to track the provenance of raw materials, verify the authenticity of sustainability claims, and ensure

compliance with regulatory requirements.

Innovative Solutions and Best Practices
As companies strive to stay ahead of the curve in sustainable management, they are adopting innovative solutions and best practices that drive continuous improvement. Future trends in this area include the development of new business models, the adoption of cutting-edge technologies, and the implementation of collaborative initiatives that leverage the strengths of multiple stakeholders.

New Business Models
The shift towards sustainable management is prompting companies to rethink their business models.

- Circular economy principles, which emphasize the reuse and recycling of materials, are gaining traction as a way to reduce waste and create value.

Companies are also exploring new revenue streams through the development of sustainable products and services, as well as partnerships with other organizations to drive collective impact.

Collaborative Initiatives
Collaboration is key to achieving sustainable management goals. Companies are increasingly partnering with governments, non-profits, and other businesses to address complex sustainability challenges. These collaborative initiatives can take various forms, including public-private partnerships, industry alliances, and multi-stakeholder coalitions. By working together, organizations can pool resources, share knowledge, and drive systemic change.

The Future of Sustainable Management
The future of sustainable management is bright, with numerous opportunities for companies to enhance their environmental, social, and governance performance. By staying ahead of emerging trends and adopting innovative practices, businesses can not only improve their bottom line but also contribute to a more sustainable and equitable world.

As the landscape continues to evolve, the integration of ESG management and the growth of ESG financial assets and trading will play a pivotal role in shaping the future of sustainable management.

Real-World Success Stories: Sustaining Green Practices
In this section, we explore real-life examples of individuals and organizations that have successfully implemented long-term sustainability strategies. These stories not only demonstrate the practical application of the concepts discussed in this chapter but also provide inspiration and insights for those looking to create a lasting impact in their own sustainability efforts.

The City of Copenhagen: Pioneering Urban Sustainability
The City of Copenhagen has long been recognized as a leader in urban sustainability. Intending to become the world's first carbon-neutral capital by 2025, Copenhagen has implemented a comprehensive strategy to achieve this ambitious target. Water, light, green spaces and innovative thinking are key elements in Copenhagen's architectural development and some of the ingredients that combine sustainable actions with a high quality of life.

- Creating a Culture of Sustainability: Sustainability is a core value for the City of Copenhagen, influencing policy decisions and urban planning. The city has created a culture where citizens are actively engaged in sustainability initiatives. Public awareness campaigns and community programs encourage residents to adopt sustainable practices, such as cycling, recycling, and energy conservation.
- Continuous Monitoring and Optimization: Copenhagen continuously monitors its progress towards carbon neutrality through detailed reporting and analysis. The city has implemented a smart city framework, utilizing data and technology to optimize energy consumption, transportation, and waste management. By leveraging real-time data, Copenhagen can make informed decisions and continuously improve its sustainability efforts.
- Training and Development for Green Competencies: The City of Copenhagen invests in training and development programs to build green competencies among its workforce and citizens. Educational initiatives, such as workshops and seminars, provide individuals with the knowledge and skills needed to contribute to the city's sustainability goals. The city also collaborates with universities and research institutions to advance sustainability research and innovation.
- Building Partnerships with Green Organizations: Copenhagen collaborates with a wide range of stakeholders, including businesses, NGOs, and international organizations, to drive sustainability

initiatives. The city is a member of the C40 Cities Climate Leadership Group, which brings together cities from around the world to share best practices and collaborate on climate action. By building strong partnerships, Copenhagen leverages collective expertise and resources to achieve its sustainability goals.
- Future Trends in Sustainable Management: The City of Copenhagen is at the forefront of exploring future trends in urban sustainability. The city is investing in renewable energy sources, such as wind and solar power, and is exploring innovative solutions, such as green roofs and urban farming. Copenhagen's commitment to transparency and accountability ensures that it remains a leader in urban sustainability.
- The City of Copenhagen's journey towards carbon neutrality demonstrates the potential for cities to lead the way in sustainability. By creating a culture of sustainability, continuously monitoring and optimizing its operations, investing in training and development, building strong partnerships, and staying ahead of future trends, Copenhagen serves as a model for urban sustainability.

Conclusion: Green Practices for Long-Term Success

By embedding green practices into the core values and everyday operations, companies can ensure long-lasting environmental and financial benefits.

Continuous monitoring and optimization are essential to stay ahead of the curve, enabling organizations to adapt quickly to new challenges and opportunities.

Training and development for green competencies empower employees, fostering innovation and commitment to sustainable goals.

Building partnerships with green organizations amplifies efforts, creating a network of shared knowledge and resources that drive collective progress.

With the rise of ESG (Environmental, Social, and Governance) management and ESG financial assets, businesses have powerful tools to enhance their bottom line while promoting sustainability.

Looking ahead, staying informed about future trends in sustainable management will be critical in maintaining a competitive edge.

Key Takeaways:

1. Foster a culture of sustainability to integrate green practices into the company's DNA.
2. Implement continuous monitoring and optimization to remain agile and responsive.
3. Invest in training and development to build green competencies within your team.
4. Leverage partnerships with green organizations for mutual growth and innovation.
5. Utilize ESG management and financial assets to improve both sustainability and profitability.
6. Stay updated on future trends to anticipate and capitalize on emerging opportunities.

Actionable Advice:

- Conduct regular sustainability audits to identify areas for improvement.
- Develop a comprehensive training program focused on green skills and knowledge.
- Establish key performance indicators (KPIs) for sustainability efforts and track progress.
- Engage with industry forums and green organizations to stay informed and connected.
- Explore ESG investment opportunities to align financial growth with sustainable practices.

By implementing these strategies, businesses can not only contribute to a healthier planet but also achieve long-term success and resilience in an ever-evolving market.

As we conclude 'Green from Green II - Businesses & Utilities' it's time to reflect on the key points and consider the actionable advice that will empower you to drive meaningful change in your organization.

This book has, hopefully, provided you with a comprehensive toolkit for adopting sustainable management practices, and it is now up to you to implement these strategies and foster a culture of sustainability.

We began our journey with an introduction to the principles of sustainable management, highlighting the importance of integrating green practices into your business operations. You learned about the critical role of auditing and analyzing energy consumption, and how these foundational steps set the stage for impactful change. By understanding where your organization stands today, you can identify areas ripe for improvement, develop targeted strategies and prioritize these opportunities based on sound financial metrics.

In subsequent chapters, we explored various strategies for reducing emissions, from leveraging renewable energy sources to optimizing operational efficiencies. You should now have a basic roadmap for implementing these strategies, guided by best practices and real-world examples. Enhancing efficiency was another crucial theme, and you discovered numerous opportunities to streamline processes, reduce waste, and improve overall performance.

Sustaining green practices over the long term was a key focus of the latter chapters. Here, we emphasized the importance of developing a sustainability mindset, fostering employee engagement, and continuously monitoring and improving your practices. These sustainability 'values' must be embedded in your organizational culture to ensure that your efforts result in lasting change.

As you move forward, you might consider the following actionable advice:

- Conduct Regular Audits: Make energy audits a routine part of your operations. Regularly assess your energy consumption and identify areas for improvement.
- Set Clear Strategic Goals: Establish specific, measurable, achievable, relevant, and time-bound (SMART) goals for reducing emissions and enhancing efficiency.
- Engage Your Team: Foster a culture of sustainability by involving employees at all levels. Provide training and encourage participation in green initiatives.
- Leverage Technology: Utilize advanced technologies and data analytics to monitor energy usage and optimize performance.
- Collaborate and Learn: Stay informed about industry best practices and collaborate with other organizations to share knowledge and resources.
- Review and Adjust: Continuously review your strategies and adjust them as needed. Sustainability is an ongoing journey, not a one-time effort.

The significance of your role as a business leader, and maybe even a Green Team Leader, cannot be overstated. By implementing the strategies outlined in this book, you now have the insights to significantly reduce your organization's environmental impact and contribute to a more sustainable future. Your commitment to sustainable management will inspire others and drive broader change within your industry.

In summary, this book has equipped you with the knowledge and tools needed to lead your organization on your sustainability journey. From auditing and analysis to long-term strategy development, you now have a comprehensive playbook to guide your efforts. Take these lessons to heart, embrace your role as a green leader, and make a lasting impact on the world.

Thank you for joining us on this journey. The path forward is clear, and the responsibility is yours. Together, we can create a greener, more sustainable future.

The End

ABOUT THE AUTHOR

Jim Houlihan BEng MSc MBA CEM

Jim Houlihan is a qualified engineer with too many years of experience in offshore oil & gas, mainly in projects and international operations, and held various leadership roles in engineering and project management before moving into renewables, franchising and M&A.

During his more recent journey, Jim has acquired skills and interests that include digital marketing, data analytics, air-to-water and waste-to-energy technologies, hybrid and off-grid power and security solutions, investing in the Energy Transition and latterly, travel photography and writing.

Jim aims to help small and medium companies in developing profitable and sustainable businesses across a range of industries.

Over the years, Jim has lived and worked in Ireland, the UK, across the EU, Brazil, Southeast Asia, and Mozambique and spent a considerable time in the United States.

www.ingramcontent.com/pod-product-compliance
Lightning Source LLC
Chambersburg PA
CBHW031927240526
45464CB00023B/1869